W9-APH-016

GRACE >
IS GREATER

Copyright © 2017 City on a Hill Studio, LLC

All rights reserved. No portion of this book may be reproduced, stored in a retrieval
system, or transmitted in any form or by any means — electronic, mechanical,
photocopy, recording, scanning, or other — except for brief quotations in critical
reviews or articles, without prior written permission of the publisher.

Published in Louisville, Kentucky by City on a Hill Studio. City on a Hill Studio and
Grace is Greater are registered trademarks of City on a Hill Studio, LLC.

Additional copies of this journal along with other Grace is Greater study
resources may be purchased online at cityonahillstudio.com

Scripture quotations are taken from the HOLY BIBLE:
New International Version® Copyright © 1973, 1978, 1984 by International Bible
Society. Used by permission of Zondervan Publishing House. All rights reserved.

This journal is designed to take you deeper into the unbelievable, astonishing grace of God. Each day you'll reflect on a portion of Ephesians 2, a short section of "Grace is Greater" and additional stories, Scriptures and reflection questions to help you understand and experience grace.

TABLE OF CONTENTS

If you are *reading* "Grace is Greater" along with this journal, consider reading the corresponding chapters each week.

If you are *watching* the Grace is Greater Series, complete Week 1 after watching Episode 1, Week 2 after Episode 2, etc.

INTRODUCTION

FOR IT IS BY GRACE
YOU HAVE BEEN SAVED!

In the early 20th century, a woman named Hetty Green died, leaving behind an incredible fortune. By today's figures, it's estimated that she was worth over four billion dollars at the time of her death. She was likely the wealthiest woman in the world when she died.

What's most unusual about Hetty Green, though, is not her wealth but her stinginess. Despite her great fortune, she lived an extremely simple and miserly life. She only owned one pair of clothes. She never used heat or hot water in her house. When her son broke his leg, she refused to pay for him to go to a hospital, and his leg eventually had to be amputated. Her tightfistedness was so well known she is listed in the Guinness Book of World Records as the greatest miser in history!

Why would she live like this? Why would she, having such great wealth and resources, not live into its benefits?

Why would anyone with unlimited riches never put them to use, never enjoy them?

If you think about it, this is what we Christians do all the time! We have the abundant, amazing, outrageous, unlimited, scandalous grace of the one true God ... and yet we live as though we are impoverished orphans.

We have rejected the benefits of being a child of God for the life of an orphan.

We have inherited riches beyond our wildest imagination but continue living on our old budget, penny-pinching our way through life with God.

DON'T MISS THE GRACE OF GOD

In "Grace is Greater," Kyle Idleman quotes Hebrews 12:15:

"SEE TO IT THAT NO ONE MISSES THE GRACE OF GOD."

How could one miss the grace of God? Too often, we live like a spiritual Hetty Green: We miss the invitation to fully receive God's grace, to live as recipients of a never-ending fortune.

JOURNEY OF GRACE

My hope and prayer for you is that this journal serves as a guide to your journey in grace.

Consider making this more than just another book, another task to complete. Consider committing to a 28-day journey of grace!

This study journal has 28 days, including four days to catch up and review. That's 28 days saturated in God's grace!

Imagine what God might do in your heart and mind through this four-week journey of grace!

HOW TO USE THIS JOURNAL

DISCUSSION QUESTIONS

Each day, you'll read the selected passage twice. In the first reading, at the beginning of the day's notes, you can read to understand the content and meaning of the passage.

CONTENT AND MEANING

The goal at this point is to ask of the text, "What does it say?" and "What does it mean?" The questions under the heading "Content and Meaning" will help you reflect on the passage along these lines.

MEDITATION AND APPLICATION

Once you understand the passage's content and meaning, you'll do a second reading of the same passage. Why read the same thing again? In order to really savor the depth of the passage and to begin to apply its message to your life, you must reflect even more deeply.

The second reading is really a "second level" reading. Think of this as a level beneath the first reading. Rather than just looking at what the passage says and means, consider what it means for you and what it means for you today. So as you read the verses again, read more slowly and thoughtfully.

The goal of this second reading is meditation — to deeply engage the truths of the passage with your heart, not just your head. Biblical meditation is not like Eastern meditation, where the goal is to empty your mind. Instead, biblical mediation is about removing distractions and filling your mind with the things of God. In biblical meditation, we slow down and center ourselves on his Word.

In the sections marked "Meditation and Application," you'll ask yourself, "What does it mean for me to obey this passage today?" and "How can I love and enjoy God more as a result of these truths?"

The open space is provided to journal any thoughts prompted by the questions, or any reflections after meditating on the text. Use it as you see fit, not feeling as though you have to provide a correct answer or response to each question. ∎

BEFORE YOU BEGIN

Before diving into Day One, answer these questions.

HOW WOULD YOU CURRENTLY DEFINE GOD'S GRACE?

HOW WOULD YOU DESCRIBE GOD'S GRACE TO SOMEONE WHO DIDN'T KNOW ANYTHING ABOUT CHRISTIANITY?

WHAT IS ONE THING YOU WANT TO GET OUT OF THIS STUDY OF GOD'S GRACE?

HOW DO YOU WANT TO GROW DURING THIS JOURNEY?

 If you are watching the Grace is Greater Series, watch Episode 1 now.
Learn more at GraceIsGreaterStudy.com

WEEK 1 | GREATER THAN YOUR GUILT

DAY 1

FINDING GRACE IN EPHESIANS

IMAGINE BEING A MEMBER IN the Ephesian church when Paul's letter was read aloud. What would that have been like?

Ephesus was a large city, so the church likely gathered in numerous houses across town for worship and fellowship. New Testament expert Scot McKnight describes a typical first century church as a fellowship of about 30 members, meeting in a host's large house that would have also lodged traveling guests — like an early Airbnb rental home.

In this typical church, the gathering would include:

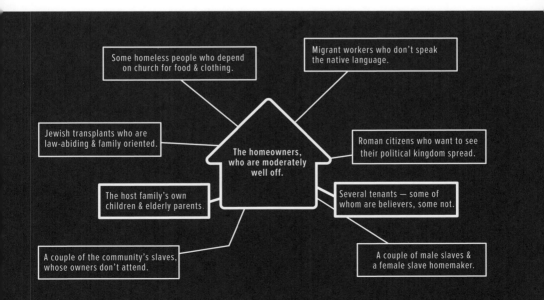

Some homeless people who depend on church for food & clothing.

Migrant workers who don't speak the native language.

Jewish transplants who are law-abiding & family oriented.

The homeowners, who are moderately well off.

Roman citizens who want to see their political kingdom spread.

The host family's own children & elderly parents.

Several tenants — some of whom are believers, some not.

A couple of the community's slaves, whose owners don't attend.

A couple of male slaves & a female slave homemaker.

The context, or the situation that a letter was written in, helps us understand the author's meaning. But this isn't merely an intellectual exercise. Imagine yourself there.

Now imagine your house's church leader has just received a copy from your church's founder, the apostle Paul. Read with fresh eyes to discover the heart of the gospel in the grace of God.

Use the space provided to underline, highlight, circle or draw anything you think is important or want to think on.

draw or write here

AS FOR YOU, YOU WERE DEAD IN YOUR TRANSGRESSIONS

AND SINS, IN WHICH YOU USED TO LIVE WHEN YOU FOLLOWED

THE WAYS OF THIS WORLD AND OF THE RULER OF THE

KINGDOM OF THE AIR, THE SPIRIT WHO IS NOW AT WORK

IN THOSE WHO ARE DISOBEDIENT. ALL OF US ALSO LIVED

AMONG THEM AT ONE TIME, GRATIFYING THE CRAVINGS OF

OUR FLESH AND FOLLOWING ITS DESIRES AND THOUGHTS.

LIKE THE REST, WE WERE BY NATURE DESERVING OF WRATH.

– EPHESIANS 2:1-3

and here!

THE EPHESIAN CHURCH

Paul was writing to a diverse group of believers who were new in their faith.

At the time of this letter's writing, Ephesus was the capital of the Roman empire. Located in modern-day Turkey, Ephesus was a busy commercial town on the edge of the Mediterranean Sea. As a port town, it was a highly secular and global place full of different types and groups of people. It was also the home to the temple of Artemis, a beloved shrine to the goddess and one of the Seven Wonders of the Ancient World.

Yet the believers in Ephesus were not so different from you and me.

Like the Ephesians, we are in desperate need of God's grace.

Like the Ephesians, our relationships were marked by a combination of friendship and conflict.
Like the Ephesians, we can easily drift into disobedience and spiritual laziness.

Like the Ephesians, we live as minorities in a secular world.

Like the Ephesians, we are children of God, having received his amazing, astonishing grace by faith in his son Jesus Christ.

When Paul describes the spiritual condition of the Ephesians apart from God, he is not suggesting they were unusually sinful or corrupt. They were simply living as unbelievers.

The message of Ephesians 2, then, is just as timely and important for us as it was for them 2,000 years ago. Paul paints a vivid contrast between what we are by nature — broken, dead in sin, drifting away — and who we are by grace.

The message of Ephesians is that God's grace is greater than our sin!

GOOD NEWS AND BAD NEWS

But before Paul gives us what I call the "Good News" about God's grace in Jesus (verses 4-10), he has to tell us the bad news (verses 1-3). The bad news is that all who are not reconciled to God and one with Christ are dead in sin. Paul describes the condition of the unbeliever in multiple ways, and in order to discover the depth of God's grace toward us in Christ, we have to understand what we are saved from.

WE ARE **DEAD**

"AS FOR YOU, YOU WERE DEAD IN YOUR TRANSGRESSIONS AND SINS."

WE ARE **DISOBEDIENT**

"YOU FOLLOWED THE WAYS OF THIS WORLD AND OF THE RULER OF THE KINGDOM OF THE AIR, THE SPIRIT WHO IS NOW AT WORK IN THOSE WHO ARE DISOBEDIENT."

WE ARE **DEPRAVED**

"ALL OF US ALSO LIVED AMONG THEM AT ONE TIME, GRATIFYING THE CRAVINGS OF OUR FLESH AND FOLLOWING ITS DESIRES AND THOUGHTS ."

WE ARE **DOOMED**

"LIKE THE REST, WE WERE BY NATURE DESERVING OF WRATH."

How does this strike you? Our spiritual condition apart from grace is not very palatable.

A BEAUTIFUL TURN

So how do we get from a place of being dead, disobedient, depraved and doomed to a place of being saved, reconciled, and restored to community?

God's grace!

That's what this study is all about. Once the Ephesians could understand their condition apart from grace, they could fully realize the lavish acceptance they had received from God!

It's not enough for us to merely understand these truths. God invites us to experience his grace against the backdrop of our need of him. ∎

QUESTIONS FOR REFLECTION

To understand how to answer these two types of questions,
see the "Questions for Reflection" on page 8.

CONTENT AND MEANING

**IN WHAT WAYS IS OUR CULTURE SIMILAR TO THE EPHESIANS' CULTURE?
HOW IS IT DIFFERENT?**

**HOW DOES THE CONTEXT OF THIS LETTER CHANGE THE WAY YOU THINK
ABOUT IT?**

**HOW CAN ONE BE BOTH "DEAD" IN THE SPIRITUAL SENSE (VERSE 1) AND
YET PHYSICALLY ALIVE?**

**WHY IS IT IMPORTANT TO UNDERSTAND OUR NEED OF GRACE BEFORE
WE LOOK AT GRACE ITSELF?**

BUT IN COVERING UP OUR SIN

WE ARE COVERING UP GRACE.

IN MINIMIZING SIN

WE ARE DIMINISHING THE

J O Y

THAT COMES WITH

FORGIVENESS.

KYLE IDLEMAN

QUESTIONS FOR REFLECTION

MEDITATION AND APPLICATION

Read Ephesians 2:1-3 again slowly and answer the following questions. To understand how to answer these types of questions, see the "Questions for Reflection" on page 8.

WHAT WOULD HAVE BEEN MOST DIFFICULT ABOUT HEARING THIS PORTION OF PAUL'S LETTER READ TO YOU? WHAT IS MOST DIFFICULT FOR YOU RIGHT NOW?

IF VERSES 1-3 MADE UP THE ENTIRETY OF PAUL'S MESSAGE TO YOU, HOW WOULD YOU FEEL? HOW WOULD YOU LIVE?

HOW IS YOUR HEART MOVED BY CONSIDERING GOD'S OUTRAGEOUS, OVERCOMING GRACE TOWARD YOU?

DAY 2

GOOD NEWS FOR DEAD PEOPLE

HAVE YOU NOTICED THE increasing fascination with zombies in the last two decades?

A zombie is "walking dead." They appear to be living, but they are dead bodies that continue to operate as if they're alive, moving through life seeking people and things to devour.

Hundreds of zombie films and novels abound, and zombie walks — organized gatherings of people dressed as the living dead — now occur in cities across the world.

Why are people so fascinated with the idea of the living dead? Perhaps it's that, on a deeper level, we are hardwired with a longing for death and resurrection.

In Ephesians 2:1-3, Paul is saying, apart from grace, you are all zombies. We are the walking dead without Christ. But in him, we have new life.

Read Ephesians 2:1-3 and use the space provided to underline, highlight, circle or draw anything you think is important or want to think on.

AS FOR YOU, YOU WERE DEAD IN YOUR TRANSGRESSIONS AND SINS, IN WHICH YOU USED TO LIVE WHEN YOU FOLLOWED THE WAYS OF THIS WORLD AND OF THE RULER OF THE KINGDOM OF THE AIR, THE SPIRIT WHO IS NOW AT WORK IN THOSE WHO ARE DISOBEDIENT. ALL OF US ALSO LIVED AMONG THEM AT ONE TIME, GRATIFYING THE CRAVINGS OF OUR FLESH AND FOLLOWING ITS DESIRES AND THOUGHTS. LIKE THE REST, WE WERE BY NATURE DESERVING OF WRATH.

— EPHESIANS 2:1-3

GOOD NEWS FOR ZOMBIES

Before God's grace, we were all zombies, following "the ways of this world and of the ruler of the kingdom of the air" (v 2).

Paul says, "As for you, you were dead in your transgressions and sins" (v 1). Not just those really bad sinners. You. And me.

APART FROM GRACE,	we are carried along by the current of the devil's schemes and lies.
	we live only for ourselves.
	we live only to gratify sinful cravings and addictions.
	we are deserving of God's wrath.
	we are the walking dead.

So what does Paul mean when he says that someone is spiritually dead from Christ?

Just as a physically dead body is unresponsive, a spiritually dead person will not be able to respond to the things of the spiritual world. Jesus says of the spiritually dead:

> THOUGH SEEING, THEY DO NOT SEE;
> THOUGH HEARING, THEY DO NOT HEAR
> OR UNDERSTAND.
>
> - MATTHEW 13:13

Those apart from God's grace can see physically but not spiritually; they can hear physically but not spiritually.

Without Christ, people are not simply sick or struggling; they are dead! And the dead don't need resuscitation; they need resurrection!

THROUGH DEATH TO LIFE

In order for a spiritually dead person to be made alive again, another death is required. Whose death is required? It's not our own!

In order for us to be made alive, God sent his own son to live the life we failed to live. Christ then went to the cross as the penalty for sins. Whose sins? Not his own — Jesus was sinless. Jesus died for our sins. Your sins, my sins. And after three days, the rock was rolled back and Jesus shook off death and walked out of the tomb. Jesus was raised to new life, and for all who believe in him, we too are resurrected!

Why would we go on living among the dead when we have been made alive and declared children of the King? ■

QUESTIONS FOR REFLECTION

CONTENT AND MEANING

WHAT MIGHT BE SOME OF THE SYMPTOMS OF BEING DEAD IN SIN? WHAT DOES SPIRITUAL LIFELESSNESS LOOK LIKE?

WHAT TYPES OF FORCES ARE PEOPLE APART FROM CHRIST SUBJECT TO? HOW HAVE YOU SEEN THESE FORCES AT WORK IN YOUR LIFE OR THE LIVES OF OTHERS?

READ ROMANS 8:11: "AND IF THE SPIRIT OF HIM WHO RAISED JESUS FROM THE DEAD IS LIVING IN YOU, HE WHO RAISED CHRIST FROM THE DEAD WILL ALSO GIVE LIFE TO YOUR MORTAL BODIES BECAUSE OF HIS SPIRIT WHO LIVES IN YOU." WHAT DOES THIS VERSE MEAN? HOW DOES IT RELATE TO OUR PASSAGE?

QUESTIONS FOR REFLECTION

MEDITATION AND APPLICATION

Read Ephesians 2:1-3 again but this time,
read more slowly and thoughtfully.

**WHAT WAS YOUR LIFE LIKE
BEFORE DISCOVERING GOD'S
GRACE?**

**WHAT WOULD YOUR LIFE BE LIKE
NOW APART FROM GOD'S GRACE?**

**HOW CAN YOU EXPRESS YOUR
GRATITUDE TO GOD FOR HIS
SAVING, RESURRECTING GRACE IN
YOUR LIFE?**

*"RELIGION WITHOUT
GRACE IS POISONOUS. A
RELATIONSHIP WITHOUT
GRACE IS POISONOUS. A
CHURCH WITHOUT GRACE
IS POISONOUS. A HEART
WITHOUT GRACE IS
POISONOUS."*

Take some time to journal your
reflections on these statements.
But don't rush to cast judgment on
others. Begin with your own heart.

**WHERE DO YOU SEE THE BITTER,
POISONOUS ROOT OF DUTY AND
EFFORT IN YOUR OWN HEART?**

**HOW DO YOU THINK YOU
DEVELOPED THIS DIFFICULTY
IN RECEIVING AND LIVING BY
GRACE?**

**NOW CONSIDER YOUR
RELATIONSHIPS: WHO IN YOUR
LIFE NEEDS SOME FORM OF
GRACE FROM GOD AND FROM
YOU?**

**CONSIDER YOUR CHURCH: HOW
CAN YOU PROMOTE A DEEPER
AWARENESS OF GRACE IN YOUR
CONGREGATION?**

DAY 3

DRIFTING AWAY

A FEW WEEKS AGO, I WAS driving my family from Louisville, Kentucky back to Columbia, Missouri — a drive we've made dozens of times. I was trying to focus on my podcast through the shouts and laughs of our three boys in the back of the van.

A fork in the highway came up, and without noticing, I drifted right onto a northbound highway headed for Chicago. About twenty minutes later, I began noticing a totally new set of buildings and landmarks. But it was only when I saw a highway marker that I realized my mistake!

I had drifted off carelessly in the wrong direction.

I didn't mean to go north, but I wasn't being attentive enough to stay on the right path. Even though it was an honest mistake, I was still left with the consequences of being in the wrong place.

Read Ephesians 2:1-3 and use the space provided to underline, highlight, circle or draw anything you think is important or want to think on.

Get creative on this page !

WRITE, DRAW, COLOR, HIGHLIGHT OR ANYTHING ELSE

AS FOR YOU, YOU WERE DEAD IN YOUR TRANSGRESSIONS AND SINS, IN WHICH YOU USED TO LIVE WHEN YOU FOLLOWED THE WAYS OF THIS WORLD AND OF THE RULER OF THE KINGDOM OF THE AIR, THE SPIRIT WHO IS NOW AT WORK IN THOSE WHO ARE DISOBEDIENT. ALL OF US ALSO LIVED AMONG THEM AT ONE TIME, GRATIFYING THE CRAVINGS OF OUR FLESH AND FOLLOWING ITS DESIRES AND THOUGHTS. LIKE THE REST, WE WERE BY NATURE DESERVING OF WRATH.

– EPHESIANS 2:1-3

FOLLOWING THE WAYS OF THE WORLD

There's a sense in which sin does this to us. Of course, we are still responsible for our sin just as I was responsible for taking the wrong highway. But sin holds a power over us, so that apart from God's grace intervening, our natural tendency is to drift onto the wrong path.

This wrong path may not be obvious at first, but the further we go, the more dangerous it becomes and the further we get from the place we need to be.

DRIFTING AS CHRISTIANS

Because our sinful nature still remains with us, we have to be careful not to drift back into sin. The author of Hebrews writes:

WE MUST PAY THE MOST CAREFUL ATTENTION, THEREFORE, TO WHAT WE HAVE HEARD, SO THAT WE DO NOT DRIFT AWAY.

HEBREWS 2:1

So how do we pay attention as believers? How do we avoid drifting away from grace and truth?

CHART: PAY ATTENTION!

1. KEEP YOUR EYES FOCUSED ON JESUS CHRIST.

HEBREWS 12:1-2

Therefore, since we are surrounded by such a great cloud of witnesses, let us throw off everything that hinders and the sin that so easily entangles. And let us run with perseverance the race marked out for us, fixing our eyes on Jesus, the pioneer and perfecter of faith. For the joy set before him he endured the cross, scorning its shame, and sat down at the right hand of the throne of God.

2. LOOK TO GOD IN THE SCRIPTURES.

PSALM 119:18

Open my eyes that I may see wonderful things in your law.

3. REMEMBER ALL GOD HAS DONE FOR YOU.

DEUTERONOMY 4:9

Only be careful, and watch yourselves closely so that you do not forget the things your eyes have seen or let them fade from your heart as long as you live. Teach them to your children and to their children after them.

4. REMAIN IN CHRISTIAN COMMUNITY.

HEBREWS 10:24-25

And let us consider how we may spur one another on toward love and good deeds, not giving up meeting together, as some are in the habit of doing, but encouraging one another — and all the more as you see the Day approaching.

5. PRAY CONTINUALLY.

MATTHEW 26:41

Watch and pray so that you will not fall into temptation. The spirit is willing, but the flesh is weak.

COME THOU FOUNT OF EVERY BLESSING

We are all quick to drift away; we're prone to wander.

Read or sing through the lyrics of "Come Thou Fount of Every Blessing" and pay special attention to verse 4.

Thankfully, God's grace is greater than our drifting.

Even though our human nature causes us to casually move toward sin, Romans 5:15 tells us that "even greater is God's wonderful grace" (NLT). How can this be?

"For the sin of one man, Adam,
caused death to rule over many.

**BUT EVEN GREATER IS GOD'S
WONDERFUL GRACE**
and his gift of righteousness, for all who receive it
will live in triumph over sin and death

THROUGH THIS ONE MAN, JESUS CHRIST."

- ROMANS 5:17 NLT-

Since Adam, sin and death have been at work in this world. But since Christ, grace and righteousness reign supreme. Grace is greater! ■

QUESTIONS FOR REFLECTION

CONTENT AND MEANING

WHAT IS THE DIFFERENCE BETWEEN RECEIVING SOMETHING AND EARNING IT? HOW DOES IT CHANGE HOW WE HOLD THE POSSESSION?

HOW DOES PAUL DESCRIBE THE EPHESIANS DRIFTING INTO SIN?

HOW DO YOU SEE OUR SOCIETY DRIFTING INTO SIN APART FROM GOD'S GRACE?

HOW CAN IT BE THAT GOD'S GRACE DOESN'T JUST CANCEL OUT OUR SIN, BUT IS ACTUALLY MUCH GREATER THAN IT?

QUESTIONS FOR REFLECTION

MEDITATION AND APPLICATION

Read Ephesians 2:1-3 again, but this time, read more slowly and thoughtfully.

HOW HAVE YOU CAUGHT YOURSELF "DRIFTING" INTO OLD WAYS OF LIFE (SEE HEBREWS 2:1)?

WHAT OLD HABITS OR PATTERNS OF LIFE REMAIN MOST TEMPTING TO YOU?

THINK BACK TO THE MOMENT OF YOUR SALVATION. WHAT WERE THE "ROAD SIGNS" THAT YOU WERE GOING IN THE WRONG DIRECTION? HOW DID YOU GET ONTO THE RIGHT PATH?

DAY 4

THE ENEMIES OF GRACE

OUR ABILITY TO APPRECIATE GRACE IS IN DIRECT CORRELATION TO THE DEGREE TO WHICH WE **ACKNOWLEDGE OUR NEED** FOR IT. THE MORE I RECOGNIZE THE UGLINESS OF MY SIN, THE MORE I CAN APPRECIATE THE BEAUTY OF GOD'S GRACE

KYLE IDLEMAN

WHEN I'M HONEST, I HAVE TO ADMIT I DON'T EVEN UNDERSTAND my sin sometimes. It seems as though it's both a force from within and a force outside of me.

Sometimes it feels as though I'm not just drifting into sin but actively being pushed into it. Could that be true?

It turns out: Grace is not without enemies.

Read Ephesians 2:1-3 and use the space provided to underline, highlight, circle or draw anything you think is important or want to think on.

draw or write here

AS FOR YOU, YOU WERE DEAD IN YOUR TRANSGRESSIONS AND SINS, IN WHICH YOU USED TO LIVE WHEN YOU FOLLOWED THE **WAYS OF THIS WORLD** AND OF THE **RULER OF THE KINGDOM OF THE AIR**, THE SPIRIT WHO IS NOW AT WORK IN THOSE WHO ARE DISOBEDIENT. ALL OF US ALSO LIVED AMONG THEM AT ONE TIME, GRATIFYING THE **CRAVINGS OF OUR FLESH** AND FOLLOWING ITS DESIRES AND THOUGHTS. LIKE THE REST, WE WERE BY NATURE DESERVING OF WRATH.

— EPHESIANS 2:1-3

THREE SPIRITUAL ENEMIES

So what makes us drift away from God and his grace? The Bible teaches that three distinct forces cause us to drift away from God: the flesh, the world, and the devil. These are the enemies of grace.

"WAYS OF THIS WORLD"

Ever since Adam sinned in the garden of Eden, we have been under a curse (Genesis 3). Our world is broken. ("World" in this sense means the collective results of the fall and the curse.)

WHAT WAS MEANT TO BE *WHOLE* IS INSTEAD *FRACTURED.*

WHAT WAS MEANT TO BE *GOOD* IS INSTEAD *CORRUPTED.*

WHAT WAS MEANT TO BE *ORDERLY* IS INSTEAD *DISORGANIZED.*

As long as we are following the ways of the world, we will move toward brokenness and death rather than God's grace and life. The world wages war against our souls.

"RULER OF THE KINGDOM OF THE AIR"

Since that original sin, the devil has a measure of power in the world. 1 Peter 5:8 says, "Your enemy the devil prowls around like a roaring lion looking for someone to devour." If it feels like someone is actively opposed to your life and holiness, it's true. The devil will one day be defeated, but until then, he is taking down as many as he can.

"CRAVINGS OF OUR FLESH"

The third enemy of grace is our own "flesh" — our hearts, minds and bodies apart from Christ. We have this inner dueling between the Spirit of God within us and our old ways and habits of life — our flesh.

When we find ourselves doing things apart from God's will and law, we are living by the flesh. Paul writes,

---

"FOR IF YOU LIVE ACCORDING TO THE FLESH, YOU WILL DIE; BUT IF BY THE SPIRIT YOU PUT TO DEATH THE MISDEEDS OF THE BODY, YOU WILL LIVE."

ROMANS 8:13

GREATER THAN THE WORLD, DEVIL AND FLESH

Although these three enemies of grace besiege us believers each day, they do not have final power over us. God's grace is greater than even these!

As Paul writes in our passage, we "used to live" under the power of these forces, but now God's Spirit dwells within us to overcome these threats.

At the return of Christ:

The world will one day be restored to its original good,

The flesh will die and we will be raised with Christ, and

The devil will be defeated for all eternity.

Though grace has its enemies in this place, one day all will be grace. ■

QUESTIONS FOR REFLECTION

CONTENT AND MEANING

HOW WOULD YOU DEFINE THE WORLD, THE DEVIL AND THE FLESH IN YOUR OWN WORDS?

WHAT OTHER PASSAGES COME TO MIND FOR EACH ONE OF THESE THREE ENEMIES OF GRACE?

HOW CAN WE KNOW FOR CERTAIN THAT ONE DAY THESE THREE FORCES AGAINST US WILL BE DEFEATED?

QUESTIONS FOR REFLECTION

MEDITATION AND APPLICATION

Read Ephesians 2:1-3 again, but this time, read more slowly and thoughtfully.

HOW HAVE YOU SEEN THESE FORCES WORKING AGAINST YOUR SPIRITUAL LIFE?
THE WORLD
THE DEVIL
THE FLESH

PERHAPS YOU ARE WEARY FROM FIGHTING AGAINST THESE FORCES. READ JESUS'S WORDS IN MATTHEW 11:28-30 AND BE ENCOURAGED TO REST IN HIM.

READ ROMANS 8:13 AGAIN. WHAT WOULD IT LOOK LIKE FOR YOU TO "BY THE SPIRIT PUT TO DEATH THE MISDEEDS OF THE BODY"?

DAY 5

GREATER THAN OUR EFFORTS

IN "GRACE IS GREATER," KYLE QUOTES BILLIONAIRE MICHAEL Bloomberg's assurance that his good deeds will get him to heaven. Bloomberg says, "When I get to heaven I'm not stopping at the gate to be interviewed. I am heading straight in. I have earned my place in heaven. It's not even close."

Kyle puts it like this:

"EVERYTHING IN ME WANTS TO DENY, COMPARE, MINIMIZE AND JUSTIFY. BUT AS LONG AS I APPROACH MY SIN WITH THAT KIND OF SPIRIT, I WON'T BE ABLE TO EXPERIENCE THE POWER AND GREATNESS OF GOD'S GRACE."

Read Ephesians 2:1-3 and use the space provided to underline, highlight, circle or draw anything you think is important or want to think on.

Get creative on this page!

AS FOR YOU, YOU WERE DEAD IN YOUR TRANSGRESSIONS AND SINS, IN WHICH YOU USED TO LIVE WHEN YOU FOLLOWED THE WAYS OF THIS WORLD AND OF THE RULER OF THE KINGDOM OF THE AIR, THE SPIRIT WHO IS NOW AT WORK IN THOSE WHO ARE DISOBEDIENT. **ALL OF US** ALSO LIVED AMONG THEM AT ONE TIME, GRATIFYING THE CRAVINGS OF OUR FLESH AND FOLLOWING ITS DESIRES AND THOUGHTS. **LIKE THE REST**, WE WERE BY NATURE DESERVING OF WRATH.

– EPHESIANS 2:1-3

Think back to the context of Ephesians we described in Day One. The letter doesn't paint a portrait of some particularly sinful person or society. Paul's point is not that the Ephesians were worse off than anyone else before Christ. These verses are simply a picture of everyday life apart from God's grace.

Paul says "all of us lived" along this sinful, corrupt path. Ephesians 2:1-3 is the condition of all people apart from the work of God.

GREATER THAN EARNING

Make a mark next to the phrase you have found yourself thinking about grace:

I deserve it because ...

- [ ] **I'M BETTER THAN OTHERS.**
- [ ] **I'M SMART ENOUGH TO PURSUE IT.**
- [ ] **I WORK HARD; I DESERVE IT.**
- [ ] **I'VE NEVER DONE ANYTHING THAT BAD.**
- [ ] **I PRAY AND READ MY BIBLE EVERY DAY TO EARN IT.**

Instead, think of God's grace as even greater than your best efforts:

GRACE

I DESERVE IT!

I CAN DO IT MYSELF!

TOO GOOD TO BE TRUE?

Could it really be that we have nothing to do to earn God's love — we simply receive it?

Consider a familiar story from the gospel of Luke (7:36-50). While Jesus was eating dinner with religious leaders, a woman "who lived a sinful life" came and stood behind him. In the presence of the son of God, she began weeping, and she washed his feet with expensive perfume and used her hair to clean them. The religious people were all looking down on this woman, so Jesus told them a parable.

> "Two people owed money to a certain moneylender. One owed him five hundred denarii and the other fifty. Neither had the money to pay him back, so he forgave the debts of both. Now which one will love him more?" (41-42).

Jesus follows this parable by telling the religious leaders that those who have been forgiven much will love much (verse 47). And to the great surprise of the room, Jesus says, "Your faith has saved you; go in peace" (verse 50).

God's grace is for anyone and everyone who will receive it. It's for those who are religious and morally hardworking. It's for the lost and sinful, who have made a wreck of their life.

For those of us who think we can earn God's favor, his grace knocks us off our feet.

One author puts it like this:

"Grace is the celebration of life, relentlessly hounding all the non-celebrants in the world. It is a floating, cosmic bash shouting its way through the streets of the universe, flinging the sweetness of its cassations to every window, pounding at every door in a hilarity beyond all liking and happening, until the prodigals come out at last and dance, and the elder brothers finally take their fingers out of their ears." ■

AMAZING GRACE

READ OR SING AND REFLECT ON
THESE WELL KNOW LYRICS.

♩ = 100

1. A - maz - ing grace! How sweet the sound That
2. 'Twas grace that taught my heart to fear, And
3. Through ma - ny dan - gers, toils and snares, I
4. The Lord has pro - mised good to me, His
5. Yea, when this flesh and heart shall fail, And

saved a wretch like me! I once was lost, but
grace my fears re - lieved; How pre - cious did that
have al - rea - dy come; 'Tis grace hath brought me
Word my hope se - cures; He will my Shield and
mor - tal life shall cease, I shall pos - sess, with -

now am found; Was blind, but now I see.
grace ap - pear The hour I first be - lieved.
safe thus far, And grace will lead me home.
Por - tion be, As long as life en - dures.
in the veil, A life of joy and peace.

6. The earth shall soon dissolve like snow,
   The sun forbear to shine;
   But God, Who called me here below,
   Shall be forever mine.

7. When we've been there ten thousand years,
   Bright shining as the sun,
   We've no less days to sing God's praise
   Than when we'd first begun.

QUESTIONS FOR REFLECTION

CONTENT AND MEANING

WHAT IS THE DIFFERENCE BETWEEN RECEIVING SOMETHING AND EARNING IT? HOW DOES IT CHANGE HOW WE HOLD THE POSSESSION?

HOW CAN IT BE THAT GOD CALLS US TO A LIFE OF OBEDIENCE AND GOOD WORKS EVEN THOUGH THIS IS NOT THE PATH OF OUR SALVATION?

WHAT IS THE PROPER MOTIVATION FOR LIVING FOR CHRIST IN ALL ASPECTS OF LIFE?

QUESTIONS FOR REFLECTION

MEDITATION AND APPLICATION

Read Ephesians 2:1-3 again, but this time, read more slowly and thoughtfully.

HOW DO YOU FIND YOURSELF CITING YOUR GOOD DEEDS AS THE GROUNDS FOR YOUR SALVATION, EVEN IF IT'S NOT THIS OBVIOUS?

HOW DO YOU THINK OF YOUR HONEST EFFORT, YOUR KNOWLEDGE OF THE BIBLE, YOUR CONCERN FOR THE POOR AND NEEDY?

COULD IT BE THAT IN YOUR SPIRITUAL LIFE, YOU STRUGGLE TO RECEIVE AND LIVE IN GOD'S GRACE?

DAY 6

WRATH AND GRACE

WE HAVE SPENT THE LAST SEVERAL DAYS CONSIDERING OUR sin, its consequences, and our need of God's grace. If you're like me, it can all be overwhelming: I know I am a sinner; just give me the Good News!

The Good News, as we said earlier, involves a measure of bad news. Today, we'll look at one final aspect of the bad news — that by nature we are deserving of God's wrath — in a way that summarizes everything you've learned so far.

God's wrath is a difficult reality, but the deeper you seek to understand it, the more beautiful it becomes.

Read Ephesians 2:1-3 and use the space provided to underline, highlight, circle or draw anything you think is important or want to think on.

AS FOR YOU, YOU WERE DEAD IN YOUR TRANSGRESSIONS AND
SINS, IN WHICH YOU USED TO LIVE WHEN YOU FOLLOWED THE
WAYS OF THIS WORLD AND OF THE RULER OF THE KINGDOM
OF THE AIR, THE SPIRIT WHO IS NOW AT WORK IN THOSE WHO
ARE DISOBEDIENT. ALL OF US ALSO LIVED AMONG THEM AT
ONE TIME, GRATIFYING THE CRAVINGS OF OUR FLESH AND
FOLLOWING ITS DESIRES AND THOUGHTS. LIKE THE REST, WE
WERE BY NATURE **DESERVING OF WRATH.**

– EPHESIANS 2:1-3

God's wrath is one of his many "attributes" — things that are true of God, his characteristics and personality. God's attributes include love, power, justice, being eternal and of course, grace.

No one attribute of God can cancel out another — that would mean there is inner division in God, and there is not. So God is full of mercy and justice; he is full of love and wrath.

God's wrath is "his love in action against sin." Because God is holy and righteous, he cannot let sin go unpunished. In other words, our actions have consequences — we do have real guilt.

Yet because he is full of love, mercy and grace, he doesn't bring his wrath to bear on us. How can that be? Jesus's sacrifice on the cross met the demands of God's wrath (because death is the penalty for sin) and the demands of God's grace (so sinners like you and me get to go free!).

As Paul puts it in his letter to the Romans:

BUT GOD DEMONSTRATES HIS OWN LOVE FOR US IN THIS: WHILE WE WERE STILL SINNERS, CHRIST DIED FOR US. SINCE WE HAVE NOW BEEN JUSTIFIED BY HIS BLOOD, HOW MUCH MORE SHALL WE BE SAVED FROM GOD'S WRATH THROUGH HIM! FOR IF, WHILE WE WERE GOD'S ENEMIES, WE WERE RECONCILED TO HIM THROUGH THE DEATH OF HIS SON, HOW MUCH MORE, HAVING BEEN RECONCILED, SHALL WE BE SAVED THROUGH HIS LIFE!

— ROMANS 5:8-10

Now that is great news!

God's love for us through Christ means we are free to come just as we are before a holy God.

God's mercy toward us in Christ means there is no longer any guilt left on us.

God's grace is greater than our guilt!

Whatever your greatest sin is, it's weaker than God's grace. To put it positively, God's grace is greater than not just your worst sin, but every sin you've ever committed, combined.

THINK ABOUT IT LIKE THIS

Think this is too good to be true? The reality is that even though we barely understand the depth of our sin, we vastly underestimate the power of God's grace!

How could our sin be greater than God and his grace? Nothing in all creation — not even the longest list of sins you can imagine — can overcome God's powerful grace.

ON THE NEXT PAGE, WRITE OUT A LIST OF YOUR SINS, FAILURES, OR HURTS TO THE RIGHT OF THE GREATER THAN SYMBOL.

GRACE

Take a few minutes to memorize the verse on the following page.

If you're not too experienced memorizing Bible verses, consider saying the verse aloud **ten times.** As you repeat it over and over, you'll find yourself learning the rhythm and flow of the verse.

But mere recitation of the verse is not the goal of Bible memorization. The goal is to deeply understand and reflect on the verse. And by taking time to understand and reflect on the verse deeply now, you may be able to keep it in your memory for years to come. ■

Ask yourself the following questions about the verse:

HOW DOES THIS VERSE SPEAK TRUTH DIRECTLY TO ME?

HOW DOES THIS VERSE CONNECT TO WHAT I'VE BEEN LEARNING THROUGH THIS STUDY JOURNAL?

HOW WOULD MY LIFE BE DIFFERENT IF I FULLY BELIEVED AND LIVED OUT THE TRUTHS OF THIS VERSE?

WHEN GOD OUR SAVIOR REVEALED HIS KINDNESS AND LOVE,

HE SAVED US,

NOT BECAUSE OF THE RIGHTEOUS THINGS WE HAD DONE, BUT BECAUSE OF HIS MERCY.

TITUS 3:4-5 NLT

QUESTIONS FOR REFLECTION

CONTENT AND MEANING

HOW WOULD YOU PUT GOD'S WRATH INTO YOUR OWN WORDS?

WRITE OUT A LIST OF GOD'S ATTRIBUTES. HOW MANY CAN YOU LIST AND WHICH SEEM MOST SIGNIFICANT?

QUESTIONS FOR REFLECTION

MEDITATION AND APPLICATION

Read these Ephesians 2:1-3 again, but this time, read more slowly and thoughtfully.

IF YOU GREW UP IN CHURCH, HOW WOULD YOU HAVE DESCRIBED GOD'S WRATH IN YOUR EARLY LIFE? HOW AND WHEN DID YOUR UNDERSTANDING OF GOD'S WRATH CHANGE?

LOOK AT YOUR LIST OF GOD'S ATTRIBUTES. WHICH ONES MOVE YOUR HEART MOST RIGHT NOW? SPEND A FEW MINUTES MEDITATING ON GOD'S ATTRIBUTES.

READ ROMANS 5:8-11 ABOVE AGAIN. HOW DOES THIS TRUTH CREATE A SENSE OF GRATITUDE AND WORSHIP WITHIN YOU?

A DEEPER UNDERSTANDING OF GOD'S WRATH AND LOVE COMPELS US TO SHARE THE GOOD NEWS WITH THOSE APART FROM CHRIST. WHO HAS GOD PLACED ON YOUR HEART?

DAY 7

REVIEW & REFLECTION

On the seventh day of each week, we're going to pause to review and reflect on the past week.

If you are behind a day or two, use this day to catch up.

If you are caught up, use this day to review the previous six days' notes — especially all the Scripture references and stories.

Based on your week's reading and reflection, answer the following questions.

WHAT WAS THE MOST SIGNIFICANT THING I LEARNED ABOUT GOD THIS WEEK?

WHAT WAS THE MOST SIGNIFICANT THING I LEARNED ABOUT THE
CHRISTIAN LIFE THIS WEEK?

WHAT WAS THE MOST SIGNIFICANT THING I LEARNED ABOUT MYSELF
THIS WEEK?

WHAT WOULD MY LIFE LOOK LIKE IF I FULLY BELIEVED AND LIVED
EVERYTHING I READ AND WROTE THIS WEEK?

If you are watching the Grace is Greater Series, watch Episode 2 now.
Learn more at GraceIsGreaterStudy.com

WEEK 2 | GREATER THAN YOUR BROKENNESS

DAY 8

HIS GREAT LOVE

IN WEEK ONE, WE FOCUSED ON THE BAD NEWS THAT PRECEDES the Good News of God's grace. As Kyle writes:

> "OUR ABILITY TO APPRECIATE GRACE IS IN DIRECT CORRELATION TO THE DEGREE TO WHICH WE ACKNOWLEDGE OUR NEED FOR IT. THE MORE I RECOGNIZE THE UGLINESS OF MY SIN, THE MORE I CAN APPRECIATE THE BEAUTY OF GOD'S GRACE."

In Week Two, we are going to dive fully into the Good News — the depths of God's grace! And unlike familiar good news/bad news jokes where the bad news comes second and outweighs the good news, God's Good News comes second and blows away the bad news!

As author Jerry Bridges writes, "The Bible ... tells us the bad news that we are in trouble with God, and then it tells us the good news that God has provided a solution that far surpasses our problem. ... In Paul's message, the Good News always outweighs the bad news."

BEFORE WE BEGIN, TAKE A MOMENT TO PRAY THAT THIS BECOMES A LIFE-CHANGING WEEK FOR YOU. YOU CAN PRAY YOUR OWN PRAYER OR USE THIS PRAYER AS A GUIDE.

Father God,

Thank you for all you have shown me about my need of you.
As I prepare to go deeper in this journey into grace,
May you open the eyes of my heart to discover the riches of your grace,
The depths of your love for me, and all that you have called me to in Christ.

In the powerful Name of Christ,
Amen.

BUT BECAUSE OF **HIS GREAT LOVE FOR US**, GOD, WHO IS RICH IN MERCY, MADE US ALIVE WITH CHRIST EVEN WHEN WE WERE DEAD IN TRANSGRESSIONS — IT IS BY GRACE YOU HAVE BEEN SAVED.

– EPHESIANS 2:4-5

HIS GREAT LOVE FOR US

In Ephesians 2:1-3, we saw that we were dead apart from God's grace — we were the walking dead. But through Christ, God makes us alive. Why does he do this?

Because of his great love for us!

The apostle Paul makes it abundantly clear that God's love is a resurrecting, overcoming love. No matter how sinful you are, no matter what choices you have made in your life, no matter how far you have run from the Father ... because of his great love for you, he hasn't given up on you!

Kyle writes:

"YOU CAN RUN AWAY AND HIDE, BUT GRACE IS RELENTLESS. GRACE WILL CHASE YOU DOWN."

Grace is relentless because of God's great love for you. Because of his love — because God is love (1 John 4:8) — the Father will stop at nothing to offer his grace to you.

TOO BROKEN FOR GRACE?

Even still, you may feel like you're too broken to receive God's grace. Surely God doesn't love me that much, you might think.

But think of it this way: How much glory does it bring to God when a broken, fractured life gets healed and restored by his grace?! As we read last week, those who have been forgiven much love much (Luke 7:47).

Kyle writes:

"WHEN A BROKEN, BUSTED, AND WRECKED LIFE COLLIDES WITH JESUS, IT'S A BEAUTIFUL THING."

Over the next week, we'll look at a number of examples and stories of broken people coming face-to-face with the grace of a loving God. May you discover, receive and be overwhelmed by this grace!

KNOWN AND LOVED

I have two great fears in life, and I think many of us share these. First, I am afraid of being truly known. "What if people find out who I really am? If others see what's really inside me, they'll surely reject me." The second fear is based on the first: I am afraid of being unloved. "How could it be," I think to myself, "that I could be completely known and still completely loved?"

I think it must be one or the other: I must hide my true self to be loved, or I must be willing to be known and risk losing the love of others.

As Kyle writes:

"Some of you think the worst thing that can happen to you is that your sins will be found out and your secrets will be exposed. … But that's not the worst thing. The worst thing that can happen is that you can go through your life and nobody knows."

But in Christ, I am both known and loved. Think about how this changes things:

	BEING UNLOVED	BEING LOVED
BEING UNKNOWN	*ALONE*	*HIDING*
BEING KNOWN	*SHAME*	*SECURE*

If I am unknown and unloved, I am totally alone.
If I am known but unloved, I will live in shame.
If I am loved but unknown, I will live in hiding.
If I am loved and known, I will be secure! ■

WHICH BOX MOST ACCURATELY
DESCRIBES YOU? HOW DID YOU
END UP THERE?

HOW DO YOU MOVE INTO THE
LOWER RIGHT BOX: KNOWN AND
LOVED?

QUESTIONS FOR REFLECTION

CONTENT AND MEANING

WHAT IS THE REASON PAUL GIVES FOR GOD OFFERING HIS GRACE TO
EACH AND EVERY ONE OF US?

God loved us first and because of this love He is rich in
mercy and made a way for us to be saved.

SINCE WE WERE "DEAD IN TRANSGRESSIONS AND SIN" (EPHESIANS 2:1)
APART FROM CHRIST, HOW IS IT THAT WE ARE "MADE ALIVE"?

~~We are not made alive apart from Christ.~~
We are made alive by the death and resurrection of
Christ.
1 Cor. 15: 1-10

QUESTIONS FOR REFLECTION

MEDITATION AND APPLICATION

Read Ephesians 2:4-5 again, but this time read it more slowly, and reflect deeply on the verses' meaning for you today.

HOW DOES IT HELP TO HAVE REFLECTED ON THE BAD NEWS — OUR GUILT BEFORE A HOLY GOD AND OUR GREAT NEED FOR FORGIVENESS — BEFORE COMING TO THE GOOD NEWS OF VERSES 4 AND 5?

TAKE A FEW MOMENTS JUST TO REFLECT ON THESE VERSES, SEEKING TO LET THEM SINK INTO YOUR HEART. HOW WOULD YOUR LIFE LOOK DIFFERENT IF YOU TRULY BELIEVED AND LIVED IN THE LIGHT OF GOD'S GREAT LOVE FOR YOU?

I would probably be filled with the power of the Holy Spirit.

HOW HAVE YOU EXPERIENCED GOD'S RELENTLESS PURSUIT OF GRACE AFTER YOU? HOW DO YOU SENSE HIM STILL CHASING AFTER YOU?

God always wants for me to draw closer to Him and allow Him to do a perfect work in me.

DAY 9

ETERNAL RICHES

TURN BACK TO THE STORY OF HETTY GREEN IN THE
Introduction. Why would someone of such great wealth live in such frugality? There is value in living simply, but Hetty seemed to live as if she was totally unaware of her riches. As a result, those around her suffered from her rejection of wealth.

In what ways do you live the same way?

In my own life, I often live as a spiritual beggar despite great eternal riches in Christ. I come to God looking for small allowances of grace and strength when a vast ocean of life-giving riches is in my personal account. My guilt was transferred to the account of Christ; his riches were transferred to my account.

How is this possible?

Get creative on this page!

BUT BECAUSE OF HIS GREAT LOVE FOR US, GOD, **WHO IS RICH IN MERCY**, MADE US ALIVE WITH CHRIST EVEN WHEN WE WERE DEAD IN TRANSGRESSIONS — IT IS BY GRACE YOU HAVE BEEN SAVED.

— EPHESIANS 2:4-5

THE GOD OF ETERNAL RICHES

A life of spiritual wealth is available to us because God "is rich in mercy" (verse 4) and loves us dearly.

The Scriptures are full of references to the incredible wealth of God. According to Psalm 50, God needs nothing from us, "for every animal of the forest is mine, and the cattle on a thousand hills" (Ps. 50:10). He doesn't need us; everything is from him and for him. God does not operate in scarcity — a lack of resources — but in abundance. He is abundant in power, knowledge, glory and holiness.

But God is not just wealthy he is generous in his wealth. He doesn't hold the abundance to himself but gives freely to those he loves. God is also abundant in mercy, patience, love and grace.

Of course, we're not talking about earthly wealth — that's never guaranteed in the Scriptures. God has something better in mind for us than worldly wealth that will dissolve in time. God wants us to be rich in Christ.

OUR BOUNDLESS RICHES IN CHRIST

In the following chapter, Paul writes of his mission:

THIS GRACE WAS GIVEN ME: TO PREACH TO THE GENTILES THE BOUNDLESS RICHES OF CHRIST.

-EPHESIANS 3:8

So what are these "immeasurable riches"? In the above verse, Paul is describing the gifts we receive through our salvation in Christ. In Christ, we receive:

UNION WITH CHRIST
We become one with Jesus.

FREEDOM FROM WRATH
God's wrath is removed.

FREEDOM FROM SLAVERY
We are "ransomed" and "redeemed" from a life of spiritual bondage.

RECONCILIATION TO GOD
Our relationship with God is restored.

RIGHT STANDING WITH GOD
Our sins no longer keep us out of God's presence.

ADOPTION
We are made sons and daughters of God, brothers and sisters of Christ.

OBEDIENCE AND GROWTH
God gradually makes us more like his Son.

ASSURANCE
Once joined to Christ, nothing can separate us from God's love.

CALLING AND MISSION
God joins us to the mission of his kingdom; we are given a new purpose.

In "Grace is Greater," Kyle notes that we often live with this assumption: "He's making an offer that's too good to be true."

In human terms, this offer of salvation is too good to be true — nothing on earth could offer these immeasurable riches. But in God's economy, in an eternal world where God owns the cattle on the thousand hills, we receive all of this through Jesus.

God is indeed rich in mercy. Now this is Good News!

GREATER THAN YOUR BROKENNESS

When you hear the word "broken," what comes to mind?

WRITE DOWN A FEW WORDS (FOR EXAMPLE, "BROKEN HEALTH" OR "BROKEN MARRIAGE").

Broken relationships

Do you believe that God's grace is greater than your brokenness? Could anything be stronger or more powerful than God?

Remember, because of his great love for you — not because of anything you've earned or accomplished but simply because you belong to him — he lavishes his grace on you! ■

QUESTIONS FOR REFLECTION

CONTENT AND MEANING

WHAT DOES IT MEAN THAT GOD IS "RICH IN MERCY" (VERSE 4)?

God is always willing to pour out his grace to those who do not deserve it. A good example can be that if our sin was like a lit match on the beach, God sends a tsunami to put it out.

WHAT IS THE DIFFERENCE BETWEEN THE GOSPEL OF IMMEASURABLE RICHES AND THE "PROSPERITY GOSPEL," WHICH SUGGESTS THAT GOD WANTS TO GIVE US MATERIAL WEALTH? WHY IS IT SO IMPORTANT TO DISTINGUISH BETWEEN THE TWO?

God does provide and for those who are faithful to Him will recieve riches far greater than what they can imagine, but many of the riches do not come in the form of material wealth.

READ AND REFLECT ON PSALM 50. HOW DOES THE WEALTH AND ABUNDANCE OF GOD CHANGE THE WAY YOU UNDERSTAND HIM?

QUESTIONS FOR REFLECTION

MEDITATION AND APPLICATION

Read Ephesians 2:4-5 again, but this time read it more slowly, and reflect deeply on the verses' meaning for you today.

WHERE DO YOU FIND YOURSELF RELATING TO GOD IN A SENSE OF SPIRITUAL SCARCITY INSTEAD OF SPIRITUAL ABUNDANCE AND RICHES?

COMPARE THE LIST OF GOD'S GIFTS TO YOU (THE IMMEASURABLE RICHES) VERSUS THE LIST OF BROKENNESS. HOW DO YOU KNOW THAT GOD'S GRACE IS GREATER THAN YOUR BROKENNESS? WHAT WOULD IT LOOK LIKE TO REMEMBER THIS TRUTH ON A DAILY BASIS?

CONSIDER THE "BOUNDLESS RICHES" OF THE GOSPEL THAT COME TO US IN CHRIST. WHICH ASPECTS DO YOU LEAST UNDERSTAND? CONSIDER HOW YOU MIGHT BETTER UNDERSTAND THESE TERMS BY STUDYING EPHESIANS AND ROMANS, OR PERHAPS THROUGH A BOOK LIKE JERRY BRIDGES' "THE GOSPEL IN REAL LIFE" OR J. I. PACKER'S "CONCISE THEOLOGY."

HOW WOULD YOUR LIFE LOOK DIFFERENT IF YOU LIVED AS A DAUGHTER OR SON OF THE KING INSTEAD OF A SPIRITUAL ORPHAN? WHAT DOES THE FATHERHOOD OF GOD MEAN TO YOU TODAY?

DAY 10

MADE ALIVE

WHAT I'VE ALWAYS FOUND fascinating is that although many secular people reject the possibility of Jesus' resurrection, all people still have a deep longing for resurrection. Think about some of our most beloved stories in movies and books:

In "The Lord of the Rings" series, Gandalf sacrifices his life for others but returns to life with greater power and wisdom.

In the movie "The Matrix," Neo gets shot and seemingly dies, but a girl named Trinity kisses him and he returns to life with even more power and control of universe. At this moment, Morpheus says, "He's the one."

Maybe my favorite resurrection line comes from the movie "Robocop." The original tagline read, "A cop is resurrected as a cyborg to serve and protect."

And in case you think this is just an American fascination, you can find a whole list of British and French films, popular Indian movies and centuries-old Chinese stories with the resurrection theme at the center. Here's what all this means: There is a human impulse for life after death.

A. O. Scott, the leading movie critic at The New York Times, wrote:

"Most movies, even the most naturalistic ... are also fantasies, tapping into the unacknowledged longings and superstitions of the audience."

We are hardwired, deep within our shared humanity, to long for resurrection, for life after death.

Get creative on this page!

WRITE, DRAW, COLOR, HIGHLIGHT OR ANYTHING ELSE

BUT BECAUSE OF HIS GREAT LOVE FOR US, GOD, WHO IS RICH IN MERCY, **MADE US ALIVE WITH CHRIST** EVEN WHEN WE WERE DEAD IN TRANSGRESSIONS — IT IS BY GRACE YOU HAVE BEEN SAVED.

— EPHESIANS 2:4-5

MADE ALIVE WITH CHRIST

Some years after Ephesians was written, Paul writes the most important passage on the Resurrection to the Corinthians. In it, he extends the fact of the Resurrection in the past to the promise of a Resurrection for us in the future:

> BUT CHRIST HAS INDEED BEEN RAISED FROM THE DEAD, THE FIRSTFRUITS OF THOSE WHO HAVE FALLEN ASLEEP. FOR SINCE DEATH CAME THROUGH A MAN, THE RESURRECTION OF THE DEAD COMES ALSO THROUGH A MAN. FOR AS IN ADAM ALL DIE, SO IN CHRIST ALL WILL BE MADE ALIVE. BUT EACH IN ITS OWN TURN: CHRIST, THE FIRSTFRUITS; THEN, WHEN HE COMES, THOSE WHO BELONG TO HIM.

> — 1 CORINTHIANS 15:20-23

Did you catch that? Death entered the world through a man — Adam's one act of sin brought a lifetime of sin and brokenness on all of us. But then Life entered the world through one man — Jesus Christ, the second Adam, who lived without sin and yet was killed for the sin of others. All who follow in Adam's line follow in his death. All who follow in Christ's line follow in his Resurrection.

Jesus was raised from the dead as the firstfruits of the Resurrection. The firstfruits are those early grapes on the vine and apples on the branch; when one breaks through, it is a certainty that others will follow. A new season has begun: The winter is gone, the spring has come!

At the end of time, we too will be raised to new life — with a new, redeemed body! And it will be, like Christ's, a resurrected body free from corruption, a body immune to sickness, to cancer, to chronic pain, to depression and anxiety, a body immune to death.

No wonder we have this human impulse for life after death! It's an impulse that no movie or book can satisfy. And as C. S. Lewis put it:

_____

> "IF WE FIND OURSELVES WITH A
> DESIRE THAT NOTHING IN THIS WORLD
> CAN SATISFY, THE MOST PROBABLE
> EXPLANATION IS THAT WE WERE MADE FOR
> ANOTHER WORLD."

— C. S. LEWIS

_____

Thankfully, we were made for another world — a world of resurrection and eternity. Reflect on the lyrics of the song, New Again by Sojourn Music on the next page, and think on these two questions:

HOW DO YOU REFLECT ON THE REALITY OF A FUTURE BODILY RESURRECTION?

I think about how great it will be when that finally happens.

HOW DO YOU LOOK FORWARD TO THE DAY WHEN "THE WEAK WILL BE STRONG"?

THE SUN IT IS DAWNING,

IT PIERCES THE NIGHT,

IT CUTS THROUGH THE SHADOWS

WITH REDEMPTION'S LIGHT

The fallen will rise

The weak will be strong

DEATH TURNS TO LIFE

IN OUR SAVIOR'S ARMS.

QUESTIONS FOR REFLECTION

CONTENT AND MEANING

WHAT IS THE REASON PAUL GIVES FOR GOD'S RESURRECTING WORK IN OUR LIVES?

God's love and mercy

READ THE NARRATIVE OF THE RESURRECTION OF JESUS IN LUKE 24:1-12 AND 36-49. WHY DID THE DISCIPLES NOT EXPECT JESUS TO RISE FROM THE DEAD?

FROM LUKE 24:41: WHAT DID THE DISCIPLES FEEL IN RESPONSE TO JESUS' RESURRECTION?

QUESTIONS FOR REFLECTION

MEDITATION AND APPLICATION

Read Ephesians 2:4-5 again, but this time read it more slowly, and reflect deeply on the verses' meaning for you today.

WHERE DO YOU SEE BROKENNESS IN YOUR LIFE — YOUR HEALTH, YOUR RELATIONSHIPS, YOUR FINANCES — AND HOW DOES IT ENCOURAGE YOU THAT ONE DAY YOU WILL BE RESURRECTED TO A BRAND-NEW LIFE IN CHRIST?

CONSIDERING THE LUKE 24 NARRATIVE, IMAGINE WHAT IT WOULD HAVE BEEN LIKE TO ENCOUNTER THE RESURRECTED LORD. HOW CAN YOU EXPERIENCE JESUS IN THIS WAY TODAY THROUGH PRAYER AND WORSHIP?

HOW WOULD YOU LIVE DIFFERENTLY IF YOU KNEW THIS LIFE WAS ONLY TEMPORARY, BUT AN ETERNAL, RESURRECTED LIFE WAS AHEAD OF YOU?

DAY 11

SAVED BY GRACE

IN THE VERY BEGINNING, GOD created Adam and Eve to live in a good and complete world. They lived at peace with God, one another and their surroundings in the Garden of Eden.

But when they sinned by disobeying God's law, they were ashamed and hid themselves from him (Genesis 3:7). Of course, an all-knowing God would have known they were hiding in their nakedness, yet he still called out to them, "Where are you?" (Gen. 3:9)

Just like Adam and Eve, we suffer humiliation and shame from our own sin. But also because of Adam's sin, we live in a broken world — a world cursed to fall apart (Gen. 3:14-19). That means that we suffer the effects of brokenness even when we are not directly responsible.

As people both sinful and broken, we need the Good News. Since we are born into sin, we cannot save ourselves. Since we live in a broken world, we won't find a savior on this earth.

It is up to God to intervene then. He alone can save us. He alone can remove our guilt and shame. He alone can overcome a world of brokenness with a life-saving grace.

Get creative on this page!

BUT BECAUSE OF HIS GREAT LOVE FOR US, GOD, WHO IS RICH IN MERCY, MADE US ALIVE WITH CHRIST EVEN WHEN WE WERE DEAD IN TRANSGRESSIONS — **IT IS BY GRACE YOU HAVE BEEN SAVED.**

— EPHESIANS 2:4-5

GRACE CALLS OUT TO YOU

Adam and Eve hid from God because they assumed he surely would not love them anymore.

Kyle writes:

"SOMETIMES OUR SIN STAYS HIDDEN BECAUSE WE ARE IN DENIAL OR BECAUSE OUR PRIDE HAS BLINDED US TO IT. BUT OFTENTIMES WE TRY TO KEEP OUR SIN A SECRET BECAUSE WE JUST CAN'T DEAL WITH WHAT WE'VE DONE."

What might be hidden? In what ways might you be living as if you were still "dead in transgressions" when in reality you have been "made ... alive in Christ" (verse 5)?

Kyle continues, "You can run away and hide, but grace is relentless. Grace will chase you down."

That's exactly what happened with Adam and Eve. When God found them, he held them accountable to their sin — they had to be removed from his perfect garden. But he didn't leave them naked, ashamed and alone. He didn't send them into the wilderness to be exposed

to heat and cold and hunted by wild animals.

God gave them two things: He gave them a promise and he gave them a covering. He promised that one of their offspring would eventually defeat the devil (Gen. 3:15). They knew they would not only survive outside Eden but one day be restored to God through the victory of one of their descendants.

Second, God provided them with a covering. Since they were naked and ashamed, God covered them in the skins of animals to protect and comfort them (Gen. 3:21). But the coverings were also a sign. An animal had to be slain for Adam and Eve to be covered — for their shame to be removed.

One day their own offspring, Jesus Christ, a direct descendant of Adam's according to Matthew 1, would defeat the devil. But it wasn't the victory anyone expected. Instead, Jesus went to the cross, paying the penalty we owed. His death was in our place; "without the shedding of blood, there is no forgiveness" (Hebrews 9:22).

Just as God covered the sins of Adam and Eve with a sacrifice, he provides for our sins and brokenness with the sacrifice of his own son. ■

WHEN A
BROKEN,
BUSTED,
& WRECKED
LIFE COLLIDES
WITH JESUS,
IT'S A BEAUTIFUL
COLLISION.

- KYLE IDLEMAN -

QUESTIONS FOR REFLECTION

CONTENT AND MEANING

HOW DOES PAUL DESCRIBE THE TRANSFORMATION THAT TAKES PLACE BY GRACE IN THESE TWO VERSES?

READ GENESIS 3. WHAT STANDS OUT TO YOU AS MOST SIGNIFICANT? WHAT ARE THE SPECIFIC CURSES? HOW DO YOU SEE GRACE FORESHADOWED IN THE WORDS AND ACTIONS OF GOD?

QUESTIONS FOR REFLECTION

MEDITATION AND APPLICATION

Read Ephesians 2:4-5 again, but this time read it more slowly, and reflect deeply on the verses' meaning for you today.

DON'T BE AFRAID TO TAKE A DEEP LOOK INTO YOUR HEART. WHAT IS HIDDEN THERE? WHAT BROKENNESS IS UNKNOWN TO OTHERS?

AS LONG AS SIN AND BROKENNESS REMAIN HIDDEN IN DARKNESS, THEY HOLD A CERTAIN POWER OVER US. WHAT WOULD IT LOOK LIKE TO SHARE YOUR INNER BROKENNESS WITH A TRUSTED CHRISTIAN FRIEND OR GROUP?

REMEMBER THAT EVEN IN THE DARKNESS OF OUR HIDDEN PAINS AND BROKENNESS, CHRIST IS THE LIGHT OF THE WORLD. HE ALONE HAS THE POWER TO DRIVE OUT DARKNESS. WHAT DOES IT LOOK LIKE TO TRUST HIM TODAY?

DAY 12

GRACE FOR THE BROKEN (PART 1)

IN "GRACE IS GREATER," KYLE IDLEMAN APPLIES THE STORY OF Jesus and the Samaritan woman at the well to our own need of grace.

Before looking at the two verses for the day, take a few minutes to read John 4:1-42. Over the next two days, let's get a fuller experience of Paul's words on grace through Jesus' encounter with this woman.

BUT BECAUSE OF HIS GREAT LOVE FOR US, GOD, WHO IS RICH IN MERCY, MADE US ALIVE WITH CHRIST EVEN WHEN WE WERE DEAD IN TRANSGRESSIONS — **IT IS BY GRACE YOU HAVE BEEN SAVED.**

— EPHESIANS 2:4-5

THE BROKEN WOMAN AT THE WELL

Imagine yourself as a bystander during Jesus' conversation with the Samaritan woman at the well.

You know that Galileans like Jesus and Samaritans like this woman don't get along. You know it is against tradition for a man and a woman to have a casual conversation like this. You know that it is highly unorthodox for a spiritual and religious teacher to build a relationship with a sinful, divorced woman. From the beginning to the end, this is an unusual encounter!

As the Samaritan woman is waiting at the well — a common gathering place for women as they gather water during the day — Jesus approaches, sits down in the heat of the day, and asks her for a drink. But the conversation doesn't remain casual for long, as Jesus quickly proclaims:

> IF YOU KNEW THE GIFT OF GOD AND WHO IT IS THAT ASKS YOU FOR A DRINK, YOU WOULD HAVE ASKED HIM AND HE WOULD HAVE GIVEN YOU LIVING WATER.
>
> – JOHN 4:10

It's a very unusual statement, and when the woman asks if Jesus is talking about real water, he intensifies his claim:

> EVERYONE WHO DRINKS THIS WATER WILL BE THIRSTY AGAIN, BUT WHOEVER DRINKS THE WATER I GIVE THEM WILL NEVER THIRST. INDEED, THE WATER I GIVE THEM WILL BECOME IN THEM A SPRING OF WATER WELLING UP TO ETERNAL LIFE.
>
> – JOHN 4:13

Realizing Jesus is identifying a great spiritual thirst within her, the Samaritan woman responds, "Sir, give me this water" (John 4:14).

If only it was this simple! This woman, like many of us, wants spiritual life and healing on her own terms. We all want the benefits of Jesus' offer here and now, without a collision of his holiness and our own brokenness. We want the Good News without the bad news first.

Jesus continues,

> "GO, CALL YOUR HUSBAND. ... YOU ARE RIGHT WHEN YOU SAY THAT YOU HAVE NO HUSBAND. THE FACT IS, YOU HAVE HAD FIVE HUSBANDS, AND THE MAN YOU NOW HAVE IS NOT YOUR HUSBAND."

> *- JOHN 4:16, 18*

Ouch!

Jesus goes straight for her heart! But when Jesus confronts our sin, he does so not to intensify our shame but to remove it. Although the woman tries to change the subject to an impersonal religious question, Jesus keeps the focus on her heart (John 4:19-22).

As Kyle writes, "Before we collide with the grace of God, we must collide with the truth of our own sin."

THE BROKENNESS WITHIN YOU

We are just like the Samaritan woman at the well. We want our mistakes to remain hidden. We want our past to be just that — the past. What do you fear most about becoming known?

Kyle lists several common struggles: a short temper, looking at pornography, flirting with someone not our spouse, drinking or shopping beyond moderation (39). Why are we tempted to these things? Because we are broken people apart from Christ — and that brokenness remains with us even after salvation.

To fully embrace God's grace is to fully embrace our own need for that grace.

In fact, we should want to be like the Samaritan woman. She was quick to admit her thirst for living, eternal water. She pleaded with Jesus for it.

Remember our verses for today:

> But because of his great love for us, God, who is rich in mercy, made us alive with Christ even when we were dead in transgressions — it is by grace you have been saved.

"Because of his great love for us," God pursues you. He chases you down. He waits for you at the well. He knows your every failure, your every need. He knows the desires of your heart. And he still loves you and longs to resurrect you to new life.

Jesus didn't pick this woman because she was the most moral or the most salvation-ready. She was needy and lost — "dead in transgressions" in Paul's language. But Jesus focused his love on her precisely because of her need and thirst. Jesus drew this woman back to God to demonstrate the beautiful reality that "it is by grace you have been saved!"

Tomorrow we'll finish this narrative and see the culmination of God's grace for the Samaritan woman. ■

QUESTIONS FOR REFLECTION

CONTENT AND MEANING

WHAT WERE THE DIFFERENCES BETWEEN JESUS AND THIS WOMAN, AND WHY ARE THEY SIGNIFICANT?

HOW WOULD YOU DESCRIBE THE SPIRITUAL CONDITION OF THE SAMARITAN WOMAN? HOW DO YOU OBSERVE HER AS "DEAD IN TRANSGRESSIONS"?

WHY WOULD THIS NARRATIVE BE INCLUDED IN THE GOSPEL OF JOHN? WHAT WOULD THE AUTHOR WANT US TO KNOW ABOUT GOD AND HIS SALVATION THROUGH THIS STORY?

QUESTIONS FOR REFLECTION

MEDITATION AND APPLICATION

Read Ephesians 2:4-5 again, but this time read it more slowly, and reflect deeply on the verses' meaning for you today.

TAKE A FEW MOMENTS TO ACKNOWLEDGE YOUR BROKENNESS AND NEEDINESS BEFORE GOD IN PRAYER. WHAT SINS OR FEARS COME TO MIND?

READ HEBREWS 4:16: "LET US THEN APPROACH GOD'S THRONE OF GRACE WITH CONFIDENCE, SO THAT WE MAY RECEIVE MERCY AND GRACE TO HELP US IN OUR TIME OF NEED." BRING YOUR SINS AND FEARS BEFORE GOD AND SEEK HIS HEALING AND RENEWAL.

WHO IN YOUR LIFE IS SPIRITUALLY DRY AND THIRSTY, AWARE OF THEIR NEED BUT UNABLE TO FIND SALVATION THEMSELVES? HOW CAN YOU REACH OUT TO HIM OR HER AND SHARE THE GOOD NEWS OF GOD'S GRACE WITH THEM THIS WEEK?

DAY 13

GRACE FOR THE BROKEN (PART II)

READ AND REVIEW THE NARRATIVE BETWEEN JESUS AND THE Samaritan woman at Jacob's Well (John 4:1-42).

Today we'll conclude this encounter and see the lavish grace of God to us in Jesus Christ.

BUT BECAUSE OF HIS GREAT LOVE FOR US, GOD, WHO IS RICH IN MERCY, MADE US ALIVE WITH CHRIST EVEN WHEN WE WERE DEAD IN TRANSGRESSIONS — **IT IS BY GRACE YOU HAVE BEEN SAVED.**

— EPHESIANS 2:4-5

WHO IS THIS MAN?

When we left off, Jesus was pressing into the heart of the Samaritan woman. After Jesus described the woman's life of sin with supernatural accuracy, the woman tried to take the focus off her brokenness. But Jesus persists.

As their conversation continues, Jesus announces:

YET A TIME IS COMING AND HAS NOW COME WHEN THE TRUE WORSHIPERS WILL WORSHIP THE FATHER IN THE SPIRIT AND IN TRUTH, FOR THEY ARE THE KIND OF WORSHIPERS THE FATHER SEEKS. GOD IS SPIRIT, AND HIS WORSHIPERS MUST WORSHIP IN THE SPIRIT AND IN TRUTH.

- JOHN 4:23-24

The woman's response reveals that she is indeed spiritually thirsty: "I know that the Messiah (called Christ) is coming. When he comes, he will explain everything to us" (John 4:25).

Perhaps you can identify with this. The woman genuinely longs to see the coming of the Messiah but doesn't expect him to come this way. She expected a more fantastic, a more dramatic Messiah — perhaps a warrior riding on the clouds to defeat all God's enemies.

So as she looks upon this humble Jesus, this man focused directly on her heart, she does not expect such grace to confront her here.

To her great surprise, Jesus looks at her with piercing clarity and states the unbelievable: "I, the one speaking to you, am he" (John 4:26).

Imagine Jesus speaking this directly to you.

You feel like the wrong type of person for Jesus.
You feel like you've walked too far from God for him to find you.
You feel like he could never forgive the sins of your past.
You feel like you are too broken to be of any use in the kingdom.

Kyle writes:

"When God's grace and mercy collide with our shame and guilt, it's messy but it's beautiful. Jesus knows everything you ever did, but he wants to make sure you know that his grace is greater."

MANY BELIEVED BECAUSE OF HER

But Jesus didn't want just the Samaritan woman to experience this grace. He wanted her whole village to experience it. Listen to how the story ends:

> Many of the Samaritans from that town believed in him because of the woman's testimony, "He told me everything I ever did." So when the Samaritans came to him, they urged him to stay with them, and he stayed two days. And because of his words many more became believers. They said to the woman, "We no longer believe just because of what you said; now we have heard for ourselves, and we know that this man really is the Savior of the world."

> - JOHN 4:39-42

Through this woman — this ordinary, broken person from the wrong part of town — Jesus was able to offer and demonstrate his Father's grace to an entire community.

This is how grace works: It never ends with us. It's always living and active; it moves through us to the next person in need. Just when you think you're too broken for God, it turns out he was looking for you — to rescue you, and then through you, the world.

This is a grace greater than anything we could possibly imagine. God "made us alive with Christ, even when we were dead in transgressions — it is by grace you have been saved."

GRACE UPON GRACE

Read and reflect on the lyrics to "Grace Upon Grace" by Sandra McCracken.

IN EVERY STATION, NEW TRIALS AND TROUBLES

CALL FOR MORE GRACE THAN I CAN AFFORD

AND WHERE CAN I GO BUT TO MY DEAR SAVIOR

FOR MERCY THAT POURS FROM BOUNDLESS STORES.

GRACE UPON GRACE, EVERY SIN REPAIRED

EVERY VOID RESTORED, YOU WILL FIND HIM THERE.

IN EVERY TURNING HE WILL PREPARE YOU

WITH GRACE UPON GRACE.

- SANDRA McCRAKEN -

QUESTIONS FOR REFLECTION

CONTENT AND MEANING

WHAT NEW OBSERVATIONS AND REFLECTIONS DO YOU HAVE ON THE SAMARITAN WOMAN NARRATIVE BASED ON THESE PAST TWO DAYS?

IN WHAT WAYS DOES JESUS DEMONSTRATE A GREATER GRACE THAN THIS WOMAN'S GUILT AND SHAME?

HOW DO YOU THINK THIS WOMAN LIVED THE REST OF HER LIFE AFTER JESUS SPOKE TO HER?

QUESTIONS FOR REFLECTION

MEDITATION AND APPLICATION

Read Ephesians 2:4-5 again, but this time read it more slowly, and reflect deeply on the verses' meaning for you today.

HOW DO YOU SEE YOUR OWN STORY OF CHANGE IN THE SAMARITAN'S ENCOUNTER WITH CHRIST?

WHAT AREAS OF YOUR LIFE DO YOU FEEL LIKE YOU NEED TO "GET RIGHT" OR "CLEAN UP" BEFORE RECEIVING GOD'S GRACE? WHY DO YOU HAVE THIS IMPULSE?

HOW DO YOU THINK ABOUT BEING USED LIKE THE SAMARITAN WOMAN: AN EXAMPLE TO OTHERS AND A VESSEL OF GOD'S GRACE TOWARD OTHERS?

WHAT FEARS DO YOU HAVE IN SHARING YOUR STORY OF GRACE WITH YOUR FAMILY AND FRIENDS AND NEIGHBORS?

WHAT WOULD IT LOOK LIKE FOR YOU TO STEP OUT IN FAITH THIS WEEK AND SHARE YOUR TESTIMONY OR THE GOOD NEWS OF GRACE WITH SOMEONE YOU KNOW?

DAY 14

REVIEW & REFLECTION

On the seventh day of each week, we're going to pause to review and reflect on the past week.

If you are behind a day or two, use this day to catch up.

If you are caught up, use this day to review the previous six days' notes — especially all the Scripture references and stories.

Based on your week's reading and reflection, answer the following questions.

WHAT WAS THE MOST SIGNIFICANT THING I LEARNED ABOUT GOD THIS WEEK?

WHAT WAS THE MOST SIGNIFICANT THING I LEARNED ABOUT THE CHRISTIAN LIFE THIS WEEK?

WHAT WAS THE MOST SIGNIFICANT THING I LEARNED ABOUT MYSELF THIS WEEK?

WHAT WOULD MY LIFE LOOK LIKE IF I FULLY BELIEVED AND LIVED EVERYTHING I READ AND WROTE THIS WEEK?

WEEK 3 | GREATER THAN YOUR WOUNDS

DAY 15

GRACE FOR THE WOUNDED

AS PAUL CONTINUES IN THE NEXT SECTION OF EPHESIANS 2, HE begins to repeat some of his favorite themes — the resurrection, our spiritual riches and of course, grace!

This week we'll focus on the grace of God that heals our wounds and resurrects us to eternal wholeness.

AND GOD RAISED US UP WITH CHRIST AND SEATED US WITH HIM IN THE HEAVENLY REALMS IN CHRIST JESUS, IN ORDER THAT IN THE COMING AGES HE MIGHT SHOW THE INCOMPARABLE RICHES OF HIS GRACE, EXPRESSED IN HIS KINDNESS TO US IN CHRIST JESUS.

— EPHESIANS 2:6-7

WE ARE ALL WOUNDED

We are all wounded. In a basic sense, our woundedness is not the result of our sin but the effects of others' sin against us.

Consider these very basic definitions.

Sin: Personal decision to disobey God's law.

Guilt: The effects of our sin.

Brokenness: The effects of living in a broken world.

Woundedness: The effects of others' sin against us.

Shame: Feeling unlovable as a result of guilt and woundedness.

We have all, to varying degrees, been wounded by our parents, by early life experiences, by the brokenness of the world and by abuse, neglect, loss and a thousand other causes. We are victims of life in a broken, sinful world. This does not negate our own sinfulness and need of grace, but it recognizes that we don't have to repent of our wounds, just our own personal sinning.

GRACE FOR THE WOUNDED

Like our sin, guilt and shame, we bring our woundedness to the Father. We don't come for forgiveness; we come for healing.

Look again at this wonderful turn of phrase: "Grace, expressed in [God's] kindness to us in Christ Jesus" (verse 7). God's grace is expressed in loving kindness. Kindness for your wounds.

We can easily forget God's kindness to us. We can forget that we have been made right with God, united to Christ and raised to new life by the Spirit. And by forgetting these truths, we can wonder if God is truly for us.

Have you experienced this? Perhaps you feel you are too wounded for God's healing. Perhaps you feel you even need to repent of your wounds. Perhaps you wonder why a loving, all-powerful God would allow you to be wounded in the first place.

But don't forget the kindness of God's grace. You are not simply an accumulation of wounds. You are God's child, on whom he has set his grace and kindness.

How can you know this?

LOOK TO THE CROSS

Remember that there was one who was wounded on your behalf.

As 1 Peter 2:24 says:

> "HE HIMSELF BORE
> OUR SINS" IN HIS BODY
> ON THE CROSS, SO
> THAT WE MIGHT DIE
> TO SINS AND LIVE FOR
> RIGHTEOUSNESS; "BY HIS
> WOUNDS YOU HAVE BEEN
> HEALED."

- 1 PETER 2:24

Your wounds do not define you; Jesus' wounds define you. Your sins were placed on Jesus on the cross, so there can be no further need for punishment for you. In exchange, Jesus' wounds bring you healing — his righteousness is given to you.

In other words, God's grace at the cross heals your wounds!

Reflect on the words of Isaac Watts's hymn "When I Survey the Wondrous Cross." ■

WHEN I SURVEY THE WONDROUS CROSS
ON WHICH THE PRINCE OF GLORY DIED,
MY RICHEST GAIN I COUNT BUT LOSS,
AND POUR CONTEMPT ON ALL MY PRIDE.

SEE, FROM HIS HEAD, HIS HANDS, HIS FEET,
SORROW AND LOVE FLOW MINGLED DOWN.
DID E'ER SUCH LOVE AND SORROW MEET,
OR THORNS COMPOSE SO RICH A CROWN?

WERE THE WHOLE REALM OF NATURE MINE,
THAT WERE A PRESENT FAR TOO SMALL.
LOVE SO AMAZING, SO DIVINE,
DEMANDS MY SOUL, MY LIFE, MY ALL.

QUESTIONS FOR REFLECTION

CONTENT AND MEANING

HOW WOULD YOU PUT THE DIFFERENCES BETWEEN SIN, BROKENNESS AND WOUNDEDNESS IN YOUR OWN WORDS?

HOW DOES THE LIFE, DEATH AND RESURRECTION OF CHRIST PROVIDE FOR THE HUMAN NEED FOR FORGIVENESS (FROM OUR SIN) AND HEALING (FROM OUR BROKENNESS AND WOUNDEDNESS)?

QUESTIONS FOR REFLECTION

MEDITATION AND APPLICATION

Read Ephesians 2:6-7 again, but this time read it more slowly, and reflect deeply on the verses' meaning for you today.

MAKE A LIST OF THREE OR MORE WOUNDS YOU HAVE FELT IN YOUR LIFE.

MAKE A LIST OF THREE OR MORE WAYS YOU'VE EXPERIENCED THE KINDNESS OF GOD IN YOUR HURT AND WOUNDS.

WHAT DOES IT LOOK LIKE TO REFLECT ON CHRIST'S WOUNDS ON THE CROSS AS THE HEALING FOR YOUR WOUNDS? WHAT OTHER PASSAGES COME TO MIND?

HOW DO YOU RESPOND TO THE HYMN'S CLOSING LINE, THAT GOD'S LOVE DEMONSTRATED ON THE CROSS "DEMANDS MY SOUL, MY LIFE, MY ALL"?

DAY 16

RESURRECTION FOR THE WOUNDED

WE SAW IN DAY 10 THAT GOD HAS "MADE US ALIVE WITH CHRIST" (Ephesians 2:4). This is a beloved theme for Paul: He loves the resurrection so much, he comes back to it two verses later!

"And God raised us up with Christ," he exclaims, "and seated us with him in the heavenly realms" (verse 6). Why would Paul repeat this truth? Certainly he wants to emphasize again the new life we have in Christ. No amount of resurrection talk is too much for the old apostle!

AND **GOD RAISED US UP WITH CHRIST** AND SEATED US WITH HIM IN THE HEAVENLY REALMS IN CHRIST JESUS, IN ORDER THAT IN THE COMING AGES HE MIGHT SHOW THE INCOMPARABLE RICHES OF HIS GRACE, EXPRESSED IN HIS KINDNESS TO US IN CHRIST JESUS.

— EPHESIANS 2:6-7

RESURRECTED BY GRACE

When Jesus walked out of the tomb that glorious Sunday morning, you walked out with him. For all who believe, Paul says, will one day be resurrected too (1 Corinthians 15:23).

The resurrection of the saints is both a present reality in part and a future reality in full. In other words, we experience a spiritual resurrection when we put our trust in Christ — so that Paul can say in the past tense "God raised us up with Christ" (verse 6). And there is a physical resurrection in our futures — one day "We will all be changed — in a flash, in the twinkling of an eye, at the last trumpet ... the dead will be raised imperishable" (1 Cor. 15:51-52).

The resurrection that you have experience now as a believer in Christ means that you are no longer defined by your sin, brokenness and woundedness. Instead, "Death has been swallowed up in victory" (1 Cor. 15:54) and you have been "born again" (John 3). Thus your position in Christ is secure and unshakeable: God "seated us with [Christ] in the heavenly realms" (verse 6).

But you can also look forward to a final and complete resurrection in the future. One day, at the return of Christ, you will be raised to new life in a perfect, sinless, imperishable body (1 Cor. 15:50-54).

LOOKING FORWARD TO THE ETERNAL

Think about all the hurts, pains and wounds you have experienced in your life.

I think of my own journey, including losing my little sister when I was six and my older brother when I was sixteen. Those are real wounds that I carry with me to this day. As a result of this grief, I developed chronic pain and fatigue in my late teenage years and have struggled with my physical health for two decades. Additionally I have struggled with depression and discouragement through most of life — a combination of my biology and my suffering.

These are not sins that I have to repent of — they are wounds that I bring before the throne of grace for healing. And while the Lord gives significant freedom and perspective in my wounds, I must wait for the day when this broken body of mine is resurrected anew and my wounded soul is healed of its hurts.

What about you?

What wounds do you carry? Perhaps you have been severely abused, neglected or grieved. Perhaps you can see the faces of those who have caused your hurt. There is no reason to minimize, hide or repent of these wounds. But you also cannot let those wounds define you — if indeed God raised you up with Christ.

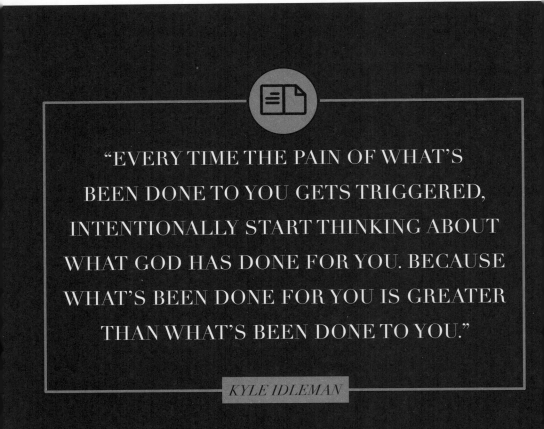

"EVERY TIME THE PAIN OF WHAT'S BEEN DONE TO YOU GETS TRIGGERED, INTENTIONALLY START THINKING ABOUT WHAT GOD HAS DONE FOR YOU. BECAUSE WHAT'S BEEN DONE FOR YOU IS GREATER THAN WHAT'S BEEN DONE TO YOU."

KYLE IDLEMAN

What wounds do you have? Write a word that represents each one in the circles below. After writing them down, take a moment to follow the arrow down to a specific phrase in Ephesians 2:4-7 that tells you who God is, and what he has promised us. Say a prayer that intentionally gives these wounds to the Father.

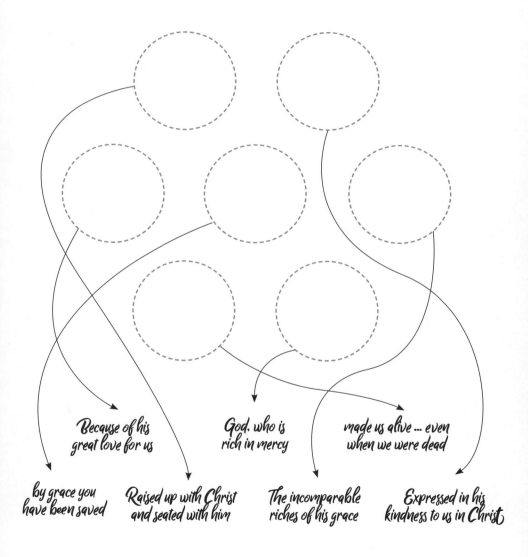

Because of his great love for us

God, who is rich in mercy

made us alive ... even when we were dead

by grace you have been saved

Raised up with Christ and seated with him

The incomparable riches of his grace

Expressed in his kindness to us in Christ

QUESTIONS FOR REFLECTION

CONTENT AND MEANING

WHY DOES PAUL DESCRIBE OUR RESURRECTION MORE THAN ONCE IN EPHESIANS 2:1-10? WHAT IS THE SIGNIFICANCE OF EACH PHRASE HE USES?

HOW CAN YOU KNOW THAT RESURRECTION IS IN YOUR FUTURE IF YOU BELIEVE IN CHRIST?

READ 1 PETER 2:24 AGAIN FROM YESTERDAY'S JOURNAL. WHAT IS THE CONNECTION BETWEEN CHRIST'S WOUNDS AND OUR RESURRECTION HOPE?

QUESTIONS FOR REFLECTION

MEDITATION AND APPLICATION

Read Ephesians 2:6-7 again, but this time read it more slowly, and reflect deeply on the verses' meaning for you today.

HOW HAS REFLECTING ON THE RESURRECTION OVER THE LAST COUPLE OF WEEKS CHANGED THE WAY YOU THINK ABOUT YOUR BROKENNESS AND WOUNDEDNESS?

HOW DO YOU RESPOND TO KYLE'S QUOTE ABOVE ABOUT FOCUSING ON WHAT'S BEEN DONE FOR YOU AS OPPOSED TO WHAT'S BEEN DONE TO YOU? HOW MIGHT THAT OUTLOOK CHANGE YOUR HURTS?

HOW MIGHT YOU SHARE WITH A TRUSTED CHRISTIAN FRIEND THIS WEEK HOW THE LORD HAS BEEN MINISTERING TO YOU IN YOUR BROKENNESS AND WOUNDEDNESS?

DAY 17

SEATED IN HEAVEN

HAVE YOU EVER BEEN TO A party or meeting and not known where to sit?

Perhaps you're at a party but know only a few people. You want to sit with them but don't want to interrupt them either; you wonder whether you should draw near or sit off at a distance until they call for you.

Or maybe it's a meeting at work: You don't want to sit too close to the boss or your supervisors and seem like you think too highly of yourself, but you also don't want to sit so far away that you seem aloof or lazy.

In these everyday situations, you've been taught that where you sit matters—your seating determines your nearness to those you're in a relationship with, those in power, and those you want to know.

In today's journal, you'll discover some something wonderful: There is already a seat for you in the heavenly realms.

Get creative on this page!

AND GOD RAISED US UP WITH CHRIST AND **SEATED US WITH HIM IN THE HEAVENLY REALMS** IN CHRIST JESUS, IN ORDER THAT IN THE COMING AGES HE MIGHT SHOW THE INCOMPARABLE RICHES OF HIS GRACE, EXPRESSED IN HIS KINDNESS TO US IN CHRIST JESUS.

— EPHESIANS 2:6-7

SEATED IN THE THRONE ROOM

We were not raised to remain under sin's control or in some uncertain spiritual place; we were raised to the right hand of the Father, next to Christ. God seats us with Christ.

How is this possible?

Remember, in salvation, we are united to Christ — made one with him.

Union with Christ means that everything that is true of him is now true of us.

Union with Christ means that whatever belongs to Christ now belongs to us.

Union with Christ means that wherever Christ sits, there is also a seat for us.

So in God's grace we can not only enter the throne room with confidence, we can also take a seat next to the King!

What does this spiritual reality mean for our living today? Paul writes in Colossians 3:1-3:

Since, then, you have been raised with Christ, set your hearts on things above, where Christ is, seated at the right hand of God. Set your minds on things above, not on earthly things. For you died, and your life is now hidden with Christ in God.

Christ is already physically where we are spiritually — "seated at the right hand of God." As a result, Paul says, "Set your minds on things above."

In other words, don't sit off at a distance; don't live for the things of earth; don't forget that you have been raised and seated in the heavenlies.

SET YOUR HEART ON THINGS ABOVE

Since God's grace is greater than our earthly needs and desires and struggles, you can set your heart on eternal things.

In your everyday challenges, in difficult relationships, God's grace is great enough for you to live like Christ.

servant (Matthew 18:21-35), the king is marked by radical generosity, and the kingdom he oversees is expected to live by the same rule of life. Similarly, since our God is "rich in mercy" (Ephesians 2:4), the church should be marked by patience, forgiveness and generosity toward one another.

As Kyle writes:

"TODAY THE CHURCH IS JESUS' COMMUNITY. AND AS OUR LEADER DEMONSTRATED THROUGH HIS ACTIONS AND REINFORCED WITH HIS TEACHINGS, OUR CORE VALUE IS GRACE. OUR CHURCHES SHOULD BE MARKED BY GRACE, FLOODED WITH GRACE KNOWN FOR GRACE."

But what about those who have caused you deep hurt? Setting your heart on things above enables you to see the sinfulness, brokenness and woundedness of those around you — and seeing those same things in yourself. When your heart is set on God, when you remember that you have an eternal seat with Christ in the heavenly realms, your position on earth becomes less defining. You can forgive others for slighting you, neglecting you, even abusing you, since you know you are not looking for this world to provide for your every need and desire.

Whether you are seated at the head of the table at the party or not — whether you are seated by the boss in the seat of honor or outside of the circle near the interns — remember that your seat in this world does not define you.

You have been raised up and seated with Christ in the throne room of God. From this eternal seat, you can extend the same mercy, forgiveness and patience that has been extended to you. ■

QUESTIONS FOR REFLECTION

CONTENT AND MEANING

DEFINE THE FOLLOWING PHRASES IN YOUR OWN WORDS: UNION WITH CHRIST, RAISED WITH CHRIST, SEATED WITH CHRIST

NOW CONSIDER THE FOLLOWING ATTRIBUTES OF GOD. HOW WOULD YOU DESCRIBE THESE IN YOUR OWN WORDS? RICH IN MERCY, QUICK TO FORGIVE, KNOWN FOR GRACE

READ THE PARABLE OF THE UNMERCIFUL SERVANT (MATTHEW 18:21-35). WHAT DO YOU LEARN ABOUT GOD FROM THIS PARABLE? WHY DO YOU THINK JESUS TOLD THIS STORY?

QUESTIONS FOR REFLECTION

MEDITATION AND APPLICATION

Read Ephesians 2:6-7 again, but this time read it more slowly, and reflect deeply on the verses' meaning for you today.

TAKE A MOMENT TO IMAGINE THE SPIRITUAL REALITY OF SITTING WITH GOD AND CHRIST. WHAT DO YOU IMAGINE? IS THIS DIFFICULT FOR YOU TO DO? WHY SO?

THINK OF A FEW FOLKS WHO HAVE HURT OR WOUNDED YOU. CONSIDER HOW THEY WERE LIKELY HURT OR WOUNDED BY SOMEONE PREVIOUSLY. WHAT DOES IT LOOK LIKE TO EXTEND THEM MERCY AND FORGIVENESS?

REFLECT ON COLOSSIANS 3:1-3. HOW MIGHT YOU SET YOUR HEART (THE CORE OF YOUR BEING, INCLUDING YOUR THOUGHTS AND FEELINGS) ON SPIRITUAL, ETERNAL REALITIES?

DAY 18

KEPT FOR LIFE

LET'S REVIEW SOME OF THE aspects of God's grace described by Paul so far in Ephesians 2:1-7.

GOD SAVED US FROM OUR SIN (VERSE 1-3).

We were disobedient, depraved and dead in sin, but God — who is rich in mercy — saved us out of that hopeless state.

GOD RAISED US FROM THE DEAD (VERSE 1, 5-6).

When we were dead in sins and transgressions, in the tomb of our sin, God made us alive again, raised us up with Christ, and blessed us with new life.

GOD LOVES US (VERSE 4).

He has done all of this out of his nature — which is love itself (1 John 4:7) — and his great affection for us as his children.

GOD SEATS US WITH CHRIST (VERSE 6).

We were not raised to remain under sin's control or in some uncertain spiritual place; we were raised to the right hand of the Father, next to Christ.

GOD KEEPS US IN CHRIST TILL THE END (VERSE 6-7).

We have been saved to a complete and eternal salvation — meaning nothing can take away the grace of God from his children.

Today, let's reflect deeply on that last aspect of God's grace toward us: We are kept in Christ till the end.

AND GOD RAISED US UP WITH CHRIST AND SEATED US WITH HIM IN THE HEAVENLY REALMS IN CHRIST JESUS, IN ORDER THAT **IN THE COMING AGES** HE MIGHT SHOW THE INCOMPARABLE RICHES OF HIS GRACE, EXPRESSED IN HIS KINDNESS TO US IN CHRIST JESUS.

— EPHESIANS 2:6-7

SECURE IN GOD'S GRACE

How can we know that once we have received God's grace, we won't fall away forever?

Author Warren Wiersbe says it like this:

"GOD'S PURPOSE IN OUR REDEMPTION IS NOT SIMPLY TO RESCUE US FROM HELL, AS GREAT A WORK AS THAT IS. HIS ULTIMATE PURPOSE IN OUR SALVATION IS THAT FOR ALL ETERNITY THE CHURCH MIGHT GLORIFY GOD'S GRACE (EPH. 1:6, 12, 14). SO, IF GOD HAS AN ETERNAL PURPOSE FOR US TO FULFILL, HE WILL KEEP US FOR ALL ETERNITY. SINCE WE HAVE NOT BEEN SAVED BY OUR GOOD WORKS, WE CANNOT BE LOST BY OUR BAD WORKS."

In other words, God isn't just saving us from something, he's saving us for something. God's plan is bigger than this world, and he wants us with him, glorifying his grace, in the eternal world to come.

But what about your ongoing sin? Don't forget: Grace is greater than your sin.

Paul writes this in Romans 8:33-35:

> WHO WILL BRING ANY CHARGE AGAINST THOSE WHOM GOD
> HAS CHOSEN? IT IS GOD WHO JUSTIFIES. WHO THEN IS THE
> ONE WHO CONDEMNS? NO ONE. CHRIST JESUS WHO DIED
> — MORE THAN THAT, WHO WAS RAISED TO LIFE — IS AT THE
> RIGHT HAND OF GOD AND IS ALSO INTERCEDING FOR US.
> WHO SHALL SEPARATE US FROM THE LOVE OF CHRIST? SHALL
> TROUBLE OR HARDSHIP OR PERSECUTION OR FAMINE OR
> NAKEDNESS OR DANGER OR SWORD?

Sure, you'll still sin, but Christ died once for all your sin — past, present and future — so it can no longer be held against you. What then could keep us from being kept by God's grace "in the coming ages"? Paul finishes his thought (Romans 8:37-39):

> NO, IN ALL THESE THINGS WE ARE MORE THAN CONQUERORS
> THROUGH HIM WHO LOVED US. FOR I AM CONVINCED THAT
> NEITHER DEATH NOR LIFE, NEITHER ANGELS NOR DEMONS,
> NEITHER THE PRESENT NOR THE FUTURE, NOR ANY POWERS,
> NEITHER HEIGHT NOR DEPTH, NOR ANYTHING ELSE IN ALL
> CREATION, WILL BE ABLE TO SEPARATE US FROM THE LOVE OF
> GOD THAT IS IN CHRIST JESUS OUR LORD.

We have been seated with Christ, and no one can take that seat from us. The work is done; the sacrifice has been accepted; the temple curtain has been torn. Our future, then, depends not on our strength but on God's — so nothing can separate us from him.

What does that mean for you today?

FORGIVENESS FOR OTHERS

In "Grace is Greater," Kyle describes a "journey of giving grace" once you know you have received grace from God.

WHERE ARE YOU ON THIS JOURNEY OF GIVING GRACE? MARK WHERE YOU ARE ON THIS JOURNEY. HOW DOES THE KNOWLEDGE THAT YOU HAVE BEEN RAISED, SEATED AND KEPT FOR ALL ETERNITY CHANGE THE WAY YOU CONSIDER FORGIVENESS AND RECONCILIATION?

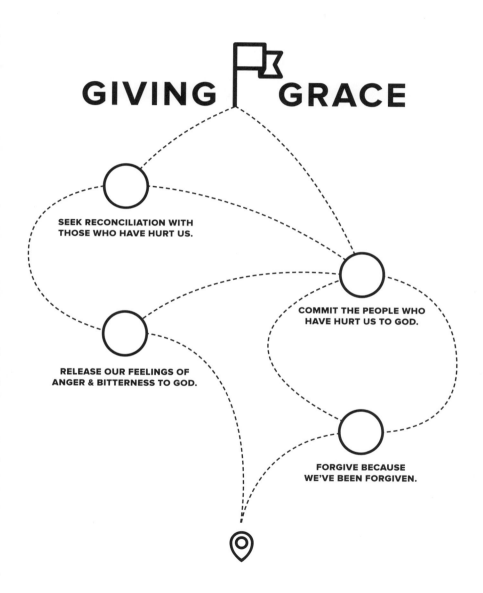

GIVING GRACE

SEEK RECONCILIATION WITH THOSE WHO HAVE HURT US.

COMMIT THE PEOPLE WHO HAVE HURT US TO GOD.

RELEASE OUR FEELINGS OF ANGER & BITTERNESS TO GOD.

FORGIVE BECAUSE WE'VE BEEN FORGIVEN.

"When forgiveness results in reconciliation it most accurately reflects God's grace and forgiveness toward us."

If you truly believed that you were secure in Christ for all eternity — that nothing on earth or in heaven could separate you from God's love — wouldn't your life be marked by grace, forgiveness and reconciliation?

PRAYER

This "journey of giving grace" may be one of the most difficult things you can do. Take a moment now to pause and pray this prayer (or create your own).

Father God,

You are good, full of love, slow to anger, abounding in grace.
You have saved me, raised me from the dead,
seated me with Christ, and promised eternal life.
Soften my heart, Father, to become like your Son.
By the power of your Holy Spirit in me,
give me the grace and strength to forgive,
to release anger, and to seek peace.
Lord God, demonstrate your love and power through me,
for the sake of your glory in the coming ages.

Amen. ■

QUESTIONS FOR REFLECTION

CONTENT AND MEANING

HOW CAN A BELIEVER IN CHRIST KNOW THAT HE OR SHE IS PROMISED
ETERNAL LIFE AND WILL BE KEPT FOREVER?

READ ROMANS 8 IN ITS ENTIRETY. HOW DOES THIS MAGNIFICENT
CHAPTER COMPLIMENT EPHESIANS 2? WHAT NEW TRUTHS ARE ADDED?

QUESTIONS FOR REFLECTION

MEDITATION AND APPLICATION

Read Ephesians 2:6-7 again, but this time read it more slowly, and reflect deeply on the verses' meaning for you today.

WHAT DOES THIS GREAT ASSUR-ANCE OF FAITH MEAN FOR YOUR LOVE FOR AND TRUST IN GOD?

HOW DO THESE GOSPEL TRUTHS PROMOTE A SPIRIT OF UNITY, FORGIVENESS AND HOPE WITHIN YOU?

HOW DOES THE PRAYER ON P.124 STRIKE YOU? CAN YOU PRAY THIS WITH HONESTY?

HOW IS GOD LEADING YOU TO STEP INTO THIS JOURNEY OF GIVING GRACE?

DAY 19

HEALED BY JESUS PART I

WE ARE ALL WOUNDED. WE LIVE IN A BROKEN WORLD, AND WE have been sinned against in severe ways. But God is a kind, loving Father. He is not just concerned with our holiness (or our lack of sinning) but also with our wholeness (our lack of brokenness).

There's no better proof of this than the life of Jesus.

AND GOD RAISED US UP WITH CHRIST AND SEATED US WITH HIM IN THE HEAVENLY REALMS IN CHRIST JESUS, IN ORDER THAT IN THE COMING AGES HE MIGHT SHOW THE INCOMPARABLE RICHES OF HIS GRACE, **EXPRESSED IN HIS KINDNESS TO US IN CHRIST JESUS.**

— EPHESIANS 2:6-7

THE LORD OF HEALING

God has expressed his kindness to us in Christ Jesus.

Consider Paul's words in the context of Jesus' healings in the gospel narratives. Jesus' healing miracles were at the center of his earthly ministry:

Jesus healed the sick.
(Matt. 12:15, 14:13-14; Luke 4:40)

Jesus healed the blind.
(Matt. 12:22; Mark 10:46-52)

Jesus healed the disabled and paralyzed.
(Matt. 9:1-8; John 5:1-13)

Jesus healed those who were possessed by demons.
(Matt. 15:21-28; Mark 1:34; Luke 8:26-39)

Jesus healed by touch and at a distance.
(Matt. 8:13)

Jesus healed on the Sabbath.
(Luke 13:10-14)

Jesus even raised the dead.
(Matt. 9:18-26; Luke 8:40-56; John 11:38-44)

All of these instances demonstrate God's "kindness to us in Christ Jesus." Let's consider one example in depth and draw out several parallels to the grace of God that overcomes our wounds.

THE HEALING OF BARTIMAEUS

One day, Jesus was teaching in Jericho.

> As Jesus and his disciples, together with a large crowd, were leaving the city, a blind man, Bartimaeus (which means "son of Timaeus"), was sitting by the roadside begging. When he heard that it was Jesus of Nazareth, he began to shout, "Jesus, Son of David, have mercy on me!" Many rebuked him and told him to be quiet, but he shouted all the more, "Son of David, have mercy on me!"
>
> — MARK 10:46-48

Notice a few things here. First, Bartimaeus is rebuked by his peers for crying out to Jesus in such a loud, obnoxious way. Those around him want him to be calm and to fit in with the crowd. But Bartimaeus, probably blind since birth, is desperate for healing. Second, notice what he screams ("Son of David, have mercy on me!") and that it is repeated twice.

The author, Mark, wants us to see that this man is physically blind but can see what others are missing: Jesus is the long-awaited Messiah, the promised one who is to sit on David's throne forever!

Jesus stopped and said, "Call him." So they called to the blind man, "Cheer up! On your feet! He's calling you." Throwing his cloak aside, he jumped to his feet and came to Jesus (Mark 10:49-50).

Notice the kindness of Jesus. He doesn't rebuke Bartimaeus like the crowd; instead, he welcomes the blind man's desperation. Indeed, he is expressing the kindness of God (Ephesians 2:7).

How does Bartimaeus respond to the Jesus' response of grace? He leaps to his feet, throws off his outer cloak, and follows Jesus' voice. What faith!

RESPONDING TO GRACE

We can pause here in the narrative and draw a few more conclusions about the grace of God and its proper response. First, grace is a healing work of God. Whether you need physical or spiritual healing — or both — you can find that healing only in and through Jesus Christ.

Second, you can live with an expectancy of God's grace. Like Bartimaeus, you can put yourself in the path of God's grace by drawing near to Jesus. You can cry out to him for healing — even if others keep telling you to accept your brokenness, to not expect healing from your woundedness. But only Bartimaeus was healed in this passage! He went after Jesus, and Jesus was happy to heal him!

Third, your response to grace matters. When Bartimaeus experiences the presence and attention of Jesus — even before his healing — he leaps to his feet. He throws off his formal outer clothing so he can get to Christ more quickly. This would have been a somewhat disgraceful act in public, but Bartimaeus — like King David many centuries before (2 Samuel 6:16-23) — is willing to suffer embarrassment to worship God in fullness!

WHAT DO YOU WANT?

As we pick up the narrative, Bartimaeus finds his way to Jesus:

> "What do you want me to do for you?" Jesus asked him. The blind man said, "Rabbi, I want to see"
> — MARK 10:51

This is an odd question for Jesus to ask of a blind man. Of course Bartimaeus wants to be healed — he's blind! But Jesus asks him anyway. "What do you want me to do for you?" Jesus wants the blind man to verbalize his need — to bring it specifically and directly to the Great Physician.

Perhaps even now, Jesus is asking you the same question: What do you want me to do for you?

If you were in the presence of Christ, what would you ask for? What do you want?

Jesus seems to be affirming that you can bring absolutely anything — however big or small — to him. You can come to him in prayer; you can come to him for healing; you can come to him running and screaming and totally undignified. He simply wants you to come. He wants to express the kindness of God to you.

"GO," SAID JESUS, "YOUR FAITH HAS HEALED YOU." IMMEDIATELY HE RECEIVED HIS SIGHT AND FOLLOWED JESUS ALONG THE ROAD.

– MARK 10:52

QUESTIONS FOR REFLECTION

CONTENT AND MEANING

READ THROUGH EACH OF THE EXAMPLES OF HEALING AT THE BEGINNING OF TODAY'S DEVOTIONAL. WHAT COMMON THEMES DO YOU SEE?

WHAT CAN WE LEARN ABOUT GOD FROM THE HEALING MINISTRY OF JESUS?

QUESTIONS FOR REFLECTION

MEDITATION AND APPLICATION

Read Ephesians 2:6-7 again, but this time read it more slowly, and reflect deeply on the verses' meaning for you today.

HOW DO YOU LONG FOR HEALING? MAKE A QUICK LIST OF THE TYPES OF HEALING YOU LONG FOR:

SPIRITUAL:

EMOTIONAL:

RELATIONAL:

PHYSICAL:

HOW HAVE YOU RESPONDED TO THE GRACE YOU HAVE ALREADY RECEIVED?

HOW WOULD YOU ANSWER THE QUESTION, IN THE PRESENCE OF CHRIST, "WHAT DO YOU WANT?"

DAY 20

HEALED BY JESUS PART II

YESTERDAY WE LOOKED AT THE HEALING ACTIVITY OF JESUS' earthly ministry. In the case of Bartimaeus, Jesus heals a man who was physically blind but had great spiritual insight.

What kind of healing are you looking for today? How do you long to see the grace of God overcome your woundedness? How do you hunger to see God's grace expressed in the kindness of Christ?

AND GOD RAISED US UP WITH CHRIST AND SEATED US WITH HIM IN THE HEAVENLY REALMS IN CHRIST JESUS, IN ORDER THAT IN THE COMING AGES HE MIGHT SHOW THE INCOMPARABLE RICHES OF HIS GRACE, **EXPRESSED IN HIS KINDNESS TO US IN CHRIST JESUS.**

— EPHESIANS 2:6-7

HEALING EVERY WOUND

Most of us aren't blind, don't have leprosy and have never been possessed by a demon. So identifying with the healing passages of the New Testament can be difficult. But the Scriptures are full of prayers for healing.

YOU CAN FIND HEALING FROM YOUR SIN — DISOBEDIENCE OF GOD'S LAW.

I said, "Have mercy on me, LORD; heal me, for I have sinned against you."
— Psalm 41:4

YOU CAN FIND HEALING FROM YOUR GUILT — THE EFFECTS OF SIN.

I have seen their ways, but I will heal them; I will guide them and restore comfort to Israel's mourners.
— Isaiah 57:18

YOU CAN FIND HEALING FROM YOUR BROKENNESS — THE EFFECTS OF LIVING IN A BROKEN WORLD.

He heals the brokenhearted and binds up their wounds.
— Psalm 147:3

YOU CAN FIND HEALING FROM YOUR WOUNDEDNESS — THE EFFECTS OF OTHERS' SIN AGAINST YOU.

Have mercy on me, LORD, for I am faint; heal me, LORD, for my bones are in agony.
— Psalm 6:2

YOU CAN FIND HEALING FROM YOUR SHAME — FEELING UNLOVABLE AS A RESULT OF GUILT AND WOUNDEDNESS.

Then your light will break forth like the dawn, and your healing will quickly appear; then righteousness will go before you, and the glory of the LORD will be your rear guard.
—Isaiah 58:8

WHAT KIND OF HEALING DO YOU SEEK? REMEMBER THE QUESTION OF JESUS:

"What do you want me to do for you?"
—Mark 10:51

There's another type of healing that Jesus wants to bring about in your life. It's the healing of your relationships.

Seeking healing in your relationships doesn't mean your wounds have to be overlooked or minimized. Instead, it means confronting your wounds and traveling the road of grace-giving.

Remember the journey of giving grace that we previously described. To fully be Christ-like in giving grace, we must learn to:

Forgive because we've been forgiven.

Release our feelings of anger and bitterness to God.

Commit the people who have hurt us to God.

Seek reconciliation with those who have hurt us.

Confronting your wounds and seeking their healing, forgiving your offender and seeking reconciliation: These are some of the most difficult things you will ever do. You may feel like you don't have the patience or strength for this journey. The road may seem too difficult.

In a sense, forgiveness is too difficult. You don't have the strength for it. But there's no reason to worry: You have also been loved, saved, forgiven, exalted and seated with Christ. You now have the very power and life of the Holy Spirit working in you!

BY HIS WOUNDS WE ARE HEALED

Wherever you are, remember the one who has made your own healing possible. Christ alone has healed you — just like he healed blind Bartimaeus.

> BUT HE WAS PIERCED FOR OUR TRANSGRESSIONS, HE WAS CRUSHED FOR OUR INIQUITIES; THE PUNISHMENT THAT BROUGHT US PEACE WAS ON HIM, AND BY HIS WOUNDS WE ARE HEALED.
>
> – ISAIAH 53:5

Christ alone can heal your wounds and restore your relationships.

DON'T CONFUSE
SIMPLE WITH EASY.
THERE'S NOTHING
EASY ABOUT THE
NEXT STEPS ON THIS
JOURNEY OF GIVING
GRACE.

IN CHRIST ALONE MY HOPE IS FOUND;

Get creative on this page!

He is my light, my strength, my song;

This cornerstone, this solid ground,

Firm through the fiercest drought and storm.

What heights of love, what depths of peace,

When fears are stilled, when strivings cease!

My comforter, my all in all —

Here in the love of Christ I stand.

QUESTIONS FOR REFLECTION

CONTENT AND MEANING

WHAT ARE THE COMMON THEMES TO THE PSALMS AND OLD TESTAMENT PRAYERS ON P.135?

HOW WOULD YOU PUT JESUS' HEALING MINISTRY—WHETHER IN THE GOSPELS OR IN OUR LIVES TODAY—INTO YOUR OWN WORDS?

WHAT TYPES OF HEALING DOES GOD PROMISE? WHAT TYPES OF HEALING ARE NOT PROMISED?

QUESTIONS FOR REFLECTION

MEDITATION AND APPLICATION

Read Ephesians 2:6-7 again, but this time read it more slowly, and reflect deeply on the verses' meaning for you today.

WHAT TYPES OF HEALING DO YOU LONG FOR TODAY?

WHO IN YOUR LIFE IS STRUGGLING FOR HOPE AND DESPERATE FOR HEALING? PRAY FOR THEM AND REACH OUT TODAY TO ENCOURAGE THEM WITH GOD'S WORD.

PICTURE SOMEONE WHO HAS HURT AND WOUNDED YOU. WHERE ARE YOU ON THE JOURNEY OF GIVING GRACE TO THEM? WHAT IS YOUR NEXT STEP?

DAY 21

REVIEW & REFLECTION

On the seventh day of each week, we're going to pause to review and reflect on the past week.

If you are behind a day or two, use this day to catch up.

If you are caught up, use this day to review the previous six days' notes — especially all the Scripture references and stories.

Based on your week's reading and reflection, answer the following questions.

WHAT WAS THE MOST SIGNIFICANT THING I LEARNED ABOUT GOD THIS WEEK?

WHAT WAS THE MOST SIGNIFICANT THING I LEARNED ABOUT THE CHRISTIAN LIFE THIS WEEK?

WHAT WAS THE MOST SIGNIFICANT THING I LEARNED ABOUT MYSELF THIS WEEK?

WHAT WOULD MY LIFE LOOK LIKE IF I FULLY BELIEVED AND LIVED EVERYTHING I READ AND WROTE THIS WEEK?

WEEK 4 | GREATER THAN YOUR WEAKNESS

DAY 22

BY GRACE — NOT BY WORKS!

AS WE JOURNEY TOGETHER INTO THE LAST WEEK IN EPHESIANS 2,
let's pause again to ask God to do more than we could even imagine
through this study on his grace.

Father God,

Thank you for what you have shown me in your Word.
Give me wisdom and insight into your glorious grace.
Open the eyes of my heart to find you in the Scriptures.
Soften my heart to see my need of grace,
And to offer it completely to those around me.
Grant me humility and persistence in my learning.

In your son's name, Amen.

FOR IT IS BY GRACE YOU HAVE BEEN SAVED, THROUGH FAITH — AND THIS IS **NOT FROM YOURSELVES**, IT IS THE GIFT OF GOD — **NOT BY WORKS**, SO THAT **NO ONE CAN BOAST**. FOR WE ARE GOD'S HANDIWORK, CREATED IN CHRIST JESUS TO DO GOOD WORKS, WHICH GOD PREPARED IN ADVANCE FOR US TO DO.

— EPHESIANS 2:8-10

IT IS BY GRACE — NOT BY WORKS!

We have already seen that Paul likes to repeat his favorite themes as a matter of emphasis. But now the old apostle gets really carried away: "It is by grace you have been saved, through faith — this is not from yourselves ... not by works ... no one can boast."

To summarize, our salvation is:

BY GRACE — NOT BY GOOD WORKS.

BY FAITH — NOT BY OBEDIENCE.

A GIFT FROM GOD — NOT FROM YOURSELVES.

THE WORK OF GOD — SO NO ONE CAN BOAST.

This one sentence (verses 8-9) is the culmination of the first seven verses to this point. It is arguably the climax of the entire book of Ephesians. And it could be the most powerful statement of Good News in the entire New Testament!

This is God's amazing grace: Through your faith in Christ — without needing any additional proof or righteousness or effort on your part — you are saved!

Do you think that you are too far from God? Your salvation is by God's grace, not by your good works.

Do you fear that your past sins cannot be wiped away? Your salvation is by faith, not obedience. Do you wonder if you have to keep up spiritually or God will reject you? Your salvation is a gift, pure and unmerited.

In short, God's grace is more powerful than your need, your brokenness, your weakness.

GRACE IN YOUR WEAKNESS

Think about it like this: Whose power is required for your salvation? If it is your power — your hard work, your obedience to the law, your good deeds — then you would have to fear losing your salvation. But if your salvation is by the power of God — his almighty strength, Christ's good deeds, the sacrifice of the cross — then your salvation is as secure as God's authority.

The ESV Study Bible notes:

"By grace refers to God's favor upon those who have transgressed his law and sinned against him. But grace may also be understood as a power in these verses. God's grace not only offers salvation but also secures it."

What does this mean, then?

The pressure is off!
You have nothing to lose.
You have nothing to prove.
Your brokenness brings wholeness.
Your woundedness is healed.
Your weakness clears the way for strength.

THE ABUNDANCE OF GRACE

One pastor tells the story of a young boy who was found on the city streets. He was clearly malnourished and taken to the hospital. When the hospital staff placed a tray of food on his lap, his eyes widened. Looking at a tall glass of milk, he asked, "Can I drink all of it?"

Clearly for this boy there was never enough of anything back home. He was used to living in poverty, and he developed a mindset of scarcity. In a place of scarcity the resources are never enough.

In a place of abundance, however, there are resources available that are more than enough. Like a vast ocean spread out in front of us, God's grace is not a limited resource.

God's grace is abundant beyond our need. ■

QUESTIONS FOR REFLECTION

CONTENT AND MEANING

WHAT ARE THE KEY WORDS OR THEMES THAT PAUL REPEATS IN EPHESIANS 2:1-10?

COMPARE THESE VERSES TO TITUS 3:4-6. HOW DO THE TWO PARAGRAPHS COMPLEMENT EACH OTHER? WHAT DID PAUL (THE AUTHOR OF BOTH BOOKS) WANT TO EMPHASIZE TO HIS READERS?

HOW DO GOD'S ATTRIBUTES (OR CHARACTERISTICS) OF GRACE AND POWER WORK TOGETHER IN SALVATION? WHAT OTHER ATTRIBUTES DO YOU SEE IN GOD THROUGH THIS PASSAGE?

QUESTIONS FOR REFLECTION

MEDITATION AND APPLICATION

Read Ephesians 2:8-10 again, but this time read it more slowly, and reflect deeply on the verses' meaning for you today.

HOW DOES THIS VISION OF GRACE DIFFER FROM WHAT YOU EXPERIENCED IN YOUR TIME AT CHURCH?

DOES ANYTHING IN YOU RESIST THIS FREE GRACE? WHY DO YOU THINK SO?

HOW DO THESE VERSES LAY
A FOUNDATION FOR OUR
CALLING TO GIVE GRACE TO ONE
ANOTHER?

HOW DO YOU RELATE TO THE BOY
WHO HAD BEEN CONDITIONED TO
THINK EVERYTHING WAS LIMITED?

HOW MIGHT YOU LIVE
DIFFERENTLY IF YOU TRULY,
DEEPLY, CONSISTENTLY BELIEVED
THAT GOD'S GRACE COVERED
YOUR ENTIRE LIFE?

DAY 23

THE STRENGTH IN YOUR WEAKNESS

WE HAVE ALREADY LOOKED AT HOW GOD'S GRACE IS GREATER than our sin, our brokenness and our woundedness. This week, from Ephesians 2:8-10, we're discovering how grace is greater even than our weakness.

Our weakness is our lack of strength to do all that God requires — to live in obedience, to demonstrate holiness and to love others perfectly. How is it that God's grace becomes strength in our weakness?

FOR IT IS BY GRACE YOU HAVE BEEN SAVED, THROUGH FAITH — AND THIS IS **NOT FROM YOURSELVES**, IT IS THE GIFT OF GOD — **NOT BY WORKS**, SO THAT **NO ONE CAN BOAST**. FOR WE ARE GOD'S HANDIWORK, CREATED IN CHRIST JESUS TO DO GOOD WORKS, WHICH GOD PREPARED IN ADVANCE FOR US TO DO.

— EPHESIANS 2:8-10

STRENGTH IN WEAKNESS

If you're like me, you may be well aware of your weakness.

I developed a chronic illness causing pain and fatigue in my late teenage years. In addition to feeling my physical weakness, I'm aware of my relational weakness: I am very conflict averse and will do almost anything to avoid a tough conversation or relationship!

Similarly, I have decades of familiarity with my spiritual weakness: The things I want to do, I cannot do consistently; the things I don't want to do — these things I do continually (Romans 7:14-20).

If it were up to my own strength (or lack thereof), my whole life would be swallowed up in weakness. But in God's grace and power, he has saved me — not through my strength, not by my good works, but in his grace, so that I cannot boast at all! God's work in my life is not just in spite of my weakness, it is through my weakness. My weakness reminds me to get out of the way and let God's strength take center stage.

What about you? How do you recognize your own weakness and need of God's power?

INHALE THE GRACE OF GOD

Perhaps the best way to be reminded of your own weakness is to consider the greatness and power of God. As you read the Scriptures and spend time in prayer, you discover how your smallness and need pale in comparison to an almighty God. But you will also discover God's grace for weak souls like you and me.

As you put yourself in the environment of God's grace, you will discover the resources needed for this journey of grace-giving we have discussed. Kyle writes:

"As you take time to inhale the oxygen of God's grace, you'll be in a place to make sure the people around you are inhaling it as well."

As you inhale grace, ask yourself, "Who needs this grace I have received?"

LEVEL-THREE FORGIVENESS

On the journey of grace-giving, Kyle writes:

"I want you to think of forgiveness on three different levels. Let's call level one forgiveness getting rid

of bitterness, anger, and rage. ... Level two forgiveness isn't so much about releasing hurt as it is releasing the person who hurt you. ... Level three forgiveness ... is a willingness to be reconciled with the person who hurt you."

Level one — getting rid of anger and bitterness — is difficult enough. When you have been offended, mistreated and hurt by someone close to you, you will discover that you don't have the strength in yourself for this step. Anger spills out as you get cut off in traffic; bitterness builds up as your mind wanders while cleaning up the house; frustration becomes visible as often as you are around your offender.

The only way to find the strength for any level of forgiveness is to embrace your weakness. Pray to the Father, "Lord, I don't have it in me to forgive this person; I'm angry and weak. I have no desire to let this frustration go. But you have forgiven me of so much; you have given me so much grace. So give me your strength to put this anger to death."

As you seek God's strength in your weakness, forgiveness and reconciliation become possible.

RECONCILED AT THE CROSS

In Colossians 1:19-22 (NLT), Paul writes this:

> FOR GOD IN ALL HIS FULLNESS WAS PLEASED TO LIVE IN CHRIST, AND THROUGH HIM GOD RECONCILED EVERYTHING TO HIMSELF. HE MADE PEACE WITH EVERYTHING IN HEAVEN AND ON EARTH BY MEANS OF CHRIST'S BLOOD ON THE CROSS.

This includes you who were once far away from God. You were his enemies, separated from him by your evil thoughts and actions. Yet now he has reconciled you to himself through the death of Christ in his physical body. As a result, he has brought you into his own presence, and you are holy and blameless as you stand before him without a single fault.

Did you catch that? God majors in forgiveness; he is in the business of reconciliation. Everything in heaven and earth now has hope for complete restoration.

Of course, you may find that level-three reconciliation is not always possible. Kyle summarizes:

"TOTAL RECONCILIATION REQUIRES BOTH FORGIVENESS FROM THE OFFENDED AND REPENTANCE FROM THE OFFENDER... THE ONE WHO HAS SINNED AGAINST YOU — WHO HAS HURT AND WOUNDED YOU — MAY NEVER FULLY REPENT. IT MAY SEEM THAT HER LEVEL OF REPENTANCE DOESN'T MATCH THE LEVEL OF OFFENSE. BUT ... OUR LEVEL OF REPENTANCE DOESN'T MATCH THE LEVEL OF OUR OFFENSE AGAINST GOD."

Your responsibility is to embrace your weakness, inhale the powerful grace of God, and exhale the fresh air of forgiveness. God may or may not enable full reconciliation.

But your soul will rest well in the all-powerful grace, a grace greater than weakness. ■

QUESTIONS FOR REFLECTION

CONTENT AND MEANING

WHAT ARE THE THREE LEVELS OF FORGIVENESS AND RECONCILIATION THAT KYLE DESCRIBES?

CONSIDER ROMANS 12:18. "AS FAR AS IT DEPENDS ON YOU, LIVE AT PEACE WITH EVERYONE." WHY DOES PAUL SAY "AS FAR AS IT DEPENDS ON YOU"?

WHY IS GOD'S STRENGTH MAGNIFIED IN THE WEAKNESS OF HIS FOLLOWERS?

QUESTIONS FOR REFLECTION

MEDITATION AND APPLICATION

Read Ephesians 2:8-10 again, but this time read it more slowly, and reflect deeply on the verses' meaning for you today.

HOW WOULD YOU DESCRIBE YOUR WEAKNESS IN THE FOLLOWING WAYS?

> PHYSICAL

> EMOTIONAL

> RELATIONAL

> SPIRITUAL

WHERE ARE YOU ON THIS THREE-LEVEL JOURNEY TOWARD RECONCILIATION? WHAT DOES IT LOOK LIKE TO PROCEED TO THE NEXT LEVEL?

READ THE COLOSSIANS 1 PASSAGE AGAIN. HOW DO YOU RECOGNIZE THAT OTHERS' SIN AGAINST YOU IS ALWAYS LESS THAN YOUR OWN OFFENSE AGAINST GOD? HOW CAN THAT REALITY MOVE YOU TO GRACE-GIVING?

DAY 24

A COMMUNITY OF GRACE

HAVE YOU NOTICED HOW MUCH of Paul's language in Ephesians is the plural tense?

All of us also lived among them at one time.

We were by nature deserving of wrath.

God, who is rich in mercy, *made us* alive with Christ.

God raised *us* up with Christ and seated us with him.

For *we* are God's handiwork. God prepared in advance for *us* to do [good works].

Based on these plural pronouns, we can understand that Paul's uses of "you" throughout the passage are plural as well. Read these as "you all" or if you're from the South, "y'all."

In other words, Paul was writing to a community, not a person. Today we'll look at the relational dynamics of Paul's words, especially that "we are God's handiwork."

FOR IT IS BY GRACE YOU HAVE BEEN SAVED, THROUGH FAITH — AND THIS IS NOT FROM YOURSELVES, IT IS THE GIFT OF GOD — NOT BY WORKS, SO THAT NO ONE CAN BOAST. **FOR WE ARE GOD'S HANDIWORK**, CREATED IN CHRIST JESUS TO DO GOOD WORKS, WHICH GOD PREPARED IN ADVANCE FOR US TO DO.

— EPHESIANS 2:8-10

THE SOCIETY OF GRACE

Writing on Ephesians, scholar John Stott says:

"NOBODY CAN EMERGE FROM A CAREFUL READING OF PAUL'S LETTER TO THE EPHESIANS WITH AN INDIVIDUAL GOSPEL. FOR EPHESIANS IS THE GOSPEL OF THE CHURCH. IT SETS FORTH GOD'S ETERNAL PURPOSE TO CREATE THROUGH JESUS CHRIST A NEW SOCIETY WHICH STANDS OUT IN BRIGHT RELIEF AGAINST THE SOMBER BACKGROUND OF THE OLD WORLD."

We are God's work. God's grace is personal and intimate, but it is not individualistic and limited. God's grace is like connective tissue in the body of Christ. Grace holds us together and strengthens us to become one.

In our highly individualistic Western culture, it is easier than ever to hold a "me and Jesus" spirituality. Yet this concept is totally absent from the New Testament.

We are not a collection of individuals. To use Stott's phrase, we are "a new society" — the society of grace.

WE ARE RELATIONAL BEINGS

Consider this: We are made in the image of a relational God. God — Father, son and Holy Spirit — has eternally existed in relationship within his being. To be made in the image of God, then, means we are created for relationship.

We are relational beings. We are hardwired to connect with others in relationships that mirror God's nature. To put it another way, we cannot be fully human without meaningful relationships.

But if we were all created for life-giving, God-like relationships, why is community so difficult? We are also weak and broken, as we have seen throughout this study. Our weakness keeps us in isolation; we find ourselves lonely and disconnected.

Is God's grace great enough for our relationships — for a new society?

ONENESS IN THE CHURCH

Paul knew that we would be too weak for this relational life. Just two chapters after our passage, he writes (Eph. 4:2-6):

> BE COMPLETELY HUMBLE AND GENTLE; BE PATIENT, BEARING WITH ONE ANOTHER IN LOVE. MAKE EVERY EFFORT TO KEEP THE UNITY OF THE SPIRIT THROUGH THE BOND OF PEACE. THERE IS ONE BODY AND ONE SPIRIT, JUST AS YOU WERE CALLED TO ONE HOPE WHEN YOU WERE CALLED; ONE LORD, ONE FAITH, ONE BAPTISM; ONE GOD AND FATHER OF ALL, WHO IS OVER ALL AND THROUGH ALL AND IN ALL.

- EPHESIANS 4:2-6

Tap into your imagination for a moment. Picture a church community where this paragraph was a reality. Imagine a congregation that is "completely humble and gentle ... patient, bearing with one another in love ... [where members] make every effort to keep the unity of the Spirit."

Don't you long for a place like this? Rather than focusing on your own faith community's shortcomings, how might you play your part in this type of church? How can you pursue oneness — one body, one Spirit, one Lord, one faith, one baptism, one Father — in the church with your brothers and sisters?

You simply cannot have a community like this without forgiveness and reconciliation.

As Paul writes to conclude his chapter on relationships in the church (Eph. 4:32):

BE KIND AND COMPASSIONATE TO ONE ANOTHER, FORGIVING EACH OTHER, JUST AS IN CHRIST GOD FORGAVE YOU.

We are relational beings, so Paul writes to our communities' weakness: Be humble; bear with one another; forgive one another.

After all, you have been forgiven of much! ■

QUESTIONS FOR REFLECTION

CONTENT AND MEANING

SCAN THROUGH THE BOOK OF EPHESIANS. WHERE ELSE DO YOU SEE THIS COMMUNITY ORIENTATION? DO YOU FIND ANY PASSAGES THAT REQUIRE INDIVIDUAL APPLICATION? WHICH PASSAGES SUGGEST COMMUNITY APPLICATION?

WHY DO YOU THINK GOD'S FOCUS IN THE SCRIPTURES IS ON HIS PEOPLE (PLURAL): ISRAEL AS A NATION AND THE CHURCH AS A NEW SOCIETY?

QUESTIONS FOR REFLECTION

MEDITATION AND APPLICATION

Read Ephesians 2:8-10 again, but this time read it more slowly, and reflect deeply on the verses' meaning for you today.

WHAT IS YOUR INITIAL RESPONSE TO THIS RELATIONAL VISION OF CHRISTIANITY? WHAT PAST HURTS OR FAILURES COME TO MIND?

WHY DO YOU THINK KEEPS MOST CHURCHES AND FAITH COMMUNITIES FALL SHORT OF PAUL'S VISION FOR RELATIONSHIPS? HOW CAN GOD'S GRACE EQUIP US FOR DEEPER LIFE TOGETHER?

PAUL SAYS, "WE ARE GOD'S HANDIWORK." WHO IN YOUR LIFE ARE YOU IN CLOSE RELATIONSHIP WITH? WHO ARE YOU WORKING ALONGSIDE TO GLORIFY GOD? MAKE A LIST OF THE BELIEVERS IN YOUR LIFE AND WRITE OUT A PRAYER FOR EACH PERSON.

DAY 25

THE GIFT OF GOD

WHEN WAS THE LAST TIME YOU watched a child open a gift?

Recently, my wife and I bought our five-year-old son a large Lego set that he had wanted for months. It wasn't his birthday; it wasn't Christmas. But he had been talking about this particular set every day and had been doing chores to save up money. His anticipation was so great we decided to buy it for him well before he could afford it himself — he likely would not have been able to buy it for months.

When he opened it he could hardly contain himself. A smile spread across his face from ear to ear. He bounced up and down and stumbled out a mess of words:

"Mom! Dad! Did you? Is this? Can I?!" He was ecstatic and spent the morning opening, assembling and playing with the new set.

But for all his joy I think my wife and I enjoyed the experience more. As a parent, I have found there are few things more fulfilling than seeing one of my children filled with joy. It's a joy to receive a gift, but when you love someone deeply, giving a gift is even more satisfying.

Today consider how salvation is the gift of God. You and I get to open and enjoy this gift — we did not earn it ourselves — but we are not the only ones filled with joy. Our Father smiles in heaven as we receive this great gift.

Get creative on this page!

FOR IT IS BY GRACE YOU HAVE BEEN SAVED, THROUGH FAITH — AND THIS IS NOT FROM YOURSELVES, **IT IS THE GIFT OF GOD** — NOT BY WORKS, SO THAT NO ONE CAN BOAST. **FOR** WE ARE GOD'S HANDIWORK, CREATED IN CHRIST JESUS TO DO GOOD WORKS, WHICH GOD PREPARED IN ADVANCE FOR US TO DO.

— EPHESIANS 2:8-10

GRACE — THE GIFT OF GOD

Our Father in heaven loves to give good gifts to his children. Jesus taught this in Matthew 7:9-11:

> WHICH OF YOU, IF YOUR SON ASKS FOR BREAD, WILL GIVE HIM A STONE? OR IF HE ASKS FOR A FISH, WILL GIVE HIM A SNAKE? IF YOU, THEN, THOUGH YOU ARE EVIL, KNOW HOW TO GIVE GOOD GIFTS TO YOUR CHILDREN, HOW MUCH MORE WILL YOUR FATHER IN HEAVEN GIVE GOOD GIFTS TO THOSE WHO ASK HIM!

If we parents give gifts to our kids out of the love in our hearts, how much more will a good and perfect Father give great things to his own children — totally by grace, demanding nothing in return!

God's grace is just that — a gift. Grace is not an award you earn, a grade you achieve or a benefit you receive for our work. No, grace is a gift, free and unmerited. All you and I do is open the gift — we receive this grace by faith.

This grace, wild and free, should produce immense joy in us. But we should also recognize the great joy it produces in our Father. Just as it pleased the Father to lead the Israelites out of slavery or as it pleased Jesus to heal the sick and blind, it brings strong joy to God to offer us this amazing gift of his grace!

GRATITUDE: RECOGNIZING GRACE

So what, then, is our role in receiving the gift of grace? We open the gift of grace by trusting Jesus and receiving salvation by faith. But we also receive grace by demonstrating gratitude to the Father.

Our English word "gratitude" comes from the Latin "gratis," meaning "a favor, free of charge, without recompense." Gratis is the root of both of our concepts of grace and thanks.

A simpler definition of gratitude could be "to recognize grace."

The wrong response to grace, then, is the opposite of gratitude: ingratitude. Ingratitude, by definition, is not recognizing grace.

Interestingly, the English use of the word "gratitude" is on the decline. According to Google Books, written mentions of "gratitude" over two hundred years suggest our culture is losing its awareness of grace.

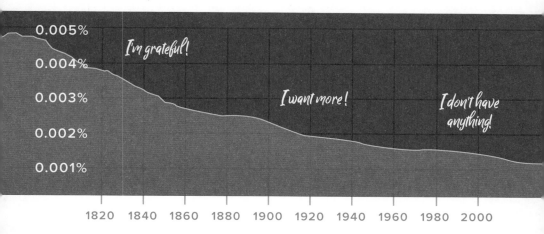

In other words, in our day and age, it is going against the grain — swimming upstream — to be grateful. What does lack of gratitude look like? Ingratitude typically spills out as complaining. Complaining is a sure what of missing grace.

Kyle writes:

"When we complain, we stop paying attention to what we have and become fixated on what we don't have. Complaining has a way of pulling the shade down on the window of grace. It keeps the light of God's grace from shining in."

God's grace is greater than your ingratitude.

Do you recognize it? ■

QUESTIONS FOR REFLECTION

CONTENT AND MEANING

CONSIDER THE ISRAELITES' GRUMBLING — THEIR COMPLAINING AND INGRATITUDE THROUGHOUT THE OLD TESTAMENT. READ EXODUS 16. HOW DOES INGRATITUDE MANIFEST ITSELF TODAY IN OUR DAY AND AGE?

IN PHILIPPIANS 2:14 PAUL COMMANDS THE CHURCH: "DO EVERYTHING WITHOUT GRUMBLING." WHAT EFFECT WOULD INGRATITUDE HAVE IN A LOCAL CHURCH? BY CONTRAST, WHAT EFFECT WOULD AN ENVIRONMENT OF GRACE AND GRATITUDE HAVE?

QUESTIONS FOR REFLECTION

MEDITATION AND APPLICATION

Read Ephesians 2:8-10 again, but this time read it more slowly, and reflect deeply on the verses' meaning for you today.

HOW HAVE YOU EXPERIENCED THE GRACE OF GOD AS A GIFT IN YOUR LIFE?

HAVE YOU CONSIDERED THE CONNECTION BETWEEN GRACE AS A GIFT AND INGRATITUDE AS A SIN BEFORE? HOW DOES THIS CHALLENGE AND ENCOURAGE YOU IN YOUR SPIRITUAL LIFE?

IDENTITY AN AREA OF YOUR LIFE WHERE YOU ARE PRONE TO COMPLAINING. HOW CAN YOU SEEK TO BE MORE GRATEFUL IN THIS AREA? HOW CAN YOU SUBMIT THIS AREA OF LIFE TO THE FATHER AND SEEK HIS GRACE?

GOD'S GRACE IS GREATER THAN OUR GRUMBLING AND INGRATITUDE. WHAT DOES THAT MEAN FOR YOU TODAY?

DAY 26

NO ONE CAN BOAST

WHEN WAS GRACE MORE REAL to you than ever?

Was it a large worship conference? Perhaps a relaxing spiritual retreat weekend? Or maybe a great sermon series at your church?

Probably not. Although these things are great channels of grace, most of us have our realest experiences of grace not in the mountaintops of life but in its valleys and caves. We experience grace most vigorously when we need it most.

In my own life I think of the hours following my brother's death in a car accident — I was desperate for God's grace to show up in my

pain and anger. I think of a season of loneliness and frustration during my college years. I think of the traumatic birth experience of one of my children — fearing for the loss of his life before he was born healthy and happy.

In each of these moments I was on my knees literally and figuratively, crying out to God in intense pain and confusion, desperate for grace to make an appearance.

These moments of profound grace have this in common: We discover grace most deeply not in the moments of our strength but in our weakness. As a result, no one can boast of receiving grace.

FOR IT IS BY GRACE YOU HAVE BEEN SAVED, THROUGH FAITH — AND THIS IS NOT FROM YOURSELVES, IT IS THE GIFT OF GOD — NOT BY WORKS, **SO THAT NO ONE CAN BOAST**. FOR WE ARE GOD'S HANDIWORK, CREATED IN CHRIST JESUS TO DO GOOD WORKS, WHICH GOD PREPARED IN ADVANCE FOR US TO DO.

— EPHESIANS 2:8-10

NO STRENGTH TO BOAST OF

To reiterate, we are all marked by weakness. We lack spiritual strength; we fail to recognize grace; we fall apart in wounded relationships in a broken world.

Even though this is a universal human experience, we typically want to hide or minimize our weakness: We say, "We're great!" even when we're falling apart. We put on our "Sunday bests" and paint a smile across our faces. We follow even our admissions of weakness with "But it's no big deal; I'll be fine!" Instead we should not only accept our weakness but boast of it. Our weakness is the canvas for God to paint the strength of his grace.

As Paul says, "It is by grace you have been saved ... so no one can boast." We can't boast of our salvation; it is entirely a work of God. Similarly, we can't boast of our spiritual growth or health; this too is a gift of God. When we boast of our spiritual life, we are minimizing and covering the grace of God. Further, we limit what God can do in and through us.

BOASTING IN YOUR WEAKNESS

God's power is manifest most fully in our weakness. As Kyle writes:

"If God's power works best in weakness, then recognizing I don't have what it takes will enable you to receive God's grace, which enables you to celebrate your weakness, which makes room for more grace to pour into your life. You get caught up in a beautiful circle of grace."

When we embrace our weakness, we put ourselves in the path of grace. When we receive grace, we become channels of its power so that others can receive grace. Grace upon grace pours into your life and overflows onto others around you.

Reflect on this classic hymn by Isaac Watts, "I Boast No More".

NO MORE, MY GOD, I BOAST NO MORE
OF ALL THE DUTIES I HAVE DONE;
I QUIT THE HOPES I HELD BEFORE,
TO TRUST THE MERITS OF THY SON

NOW, FOR THE LOSS I BEAR HIS NAME,
WHAT WAS MY GAIN I COUNT MY LOSS;
MY FORMER PRIDE I CALL MY SHAME,
AND NAIL MY GLORY TO HIS CROSS.

YES, AND I MUST AND WILL ESTEEM
ALL THINGS BUT LOSS FOR JESUS'S SAKE;
O MAY MY SOUL BE FOUND IN HIM,
AND OF HIS RIGHTEOUSNESS PARTAKE!

THE BEST OBEDIENCE OF MY HANDS
DARES NOT APPEAR BEFORE THY THRONE;
BUT FAITH CAN ANSWER THY DEMANDS,
BY PLEADING WHAT MY LORD HAS DONE.

- ISAAC WATTS -

God's grace is not just greater than our weakness. His grace finds its
home in our weakness. What great grace we receive in our time of need.
May our lives be marked by gratitude! ■

QUESTIONS FOR REFLECTION

CONTENT AND MEANING

HOW IS BOASTING OPPOSED TO THE GRACE OF GOD?

CONSIDER THE REALITY THAT NO ONE IS PERFECT IN THE SCRIPTURES EXCEPT JESUS. MOSES KILLED A MAN AND REBELLED AGAINST GOD; DAVID COMMITTED ADULTERY AND MURDER; PAUL WAS AN ANTI-CHRISTIAN TERRORIST. WHY DOES GOD RAISE UP LEADERS AND WORK THROUGH THEIR SIN AND WEAKNESS?

QUESTIONS FOR REFLECTION

MEDITATION AND APPLICATION

Read Ephesians 2:8-10 again, but this time read it more slowly, and reflect deeply on the verses' meaning for you today.

WHEN HAVE YOU MOST POWERFULLY EXPERIENCED THE GRACE OF GOD? REFLECT ON THESE MOMENTS. IN THESE EXPERIENCES, DID YOU HAVE ANY ROOM TO BOAST?

HOW HAVE YOUR EXPERIENCES OF GRACE ENABLED YOU TO ENCOURAGE AND MINISTER TO THOSE IN GREATEST NEED OF STRENGTH?

WHERE HAVE YOU SEEN EVIDENCES OF BOASTING IN WHAT GOD HAS DONE IN YOUR LIFE? WHAT DOES IT LOOK LIKE TO REPENT OF THIS AND PUT FAITH IN CHRIST'S STRENGTH DESPITE YOUR OWN WEAKNESS?

IN THE NEXT SPIRITUAL CONVERSATION YOU HAVE WITH SOMEONE, HOW MIGHT YOU POINT TO GOD'S STRONG GRACE IN THE PLACE OF YOUR WEAKNESS?

DAY 27

THE WORK OF GOD'S HANDS

AS WE COME TO THE END OF THIS STUDY JOURNAL, REFLECT ON what God has revealed to you about his grace.

You were once dead; grace made you alive again!

Your salvation is entirely by grace; you have nothing to prove!

You will be kept by God's grace for all time; the pressure is off!

You have received the gift of God's grace; you need only open and be grateful for it!

One final bit of welcome news from Paul will bring us encouragement and move us to action.

Get creative on this page!

FOR IT IS BY GRACE YOU HAVE BEEN SAVED, THROUGH FAITH — AND THIS IS NOT FROM YOURSELVES, IT IS THE GIFT OF GOD — NOT BY WORKS, SO THAT NO ONE CAN BOAST. FOR **WE ARE GOD'S HANDI-WORK, CREATED IN CHRIST JESUS TO DO GOOD WORKS**, WHICH GOD PREPARED IN ADVANCE FOR US TO DO.

— EPHESIANS 2:8-10

YOU ARE THE WORK OF GOD'S HANDS

Did you catch that? You are the work of God's hands! He created you in his own image to be like him and to work like him. In other words, you have a holy vocation.

You may hear "vocation" and immediately think of someone who works in the church for a living. Certainly that is a vocation, but every single believer has a vocation.

The word "vocation" comes from the Latin vocatio, emphasizing the "voice of God." To have a vocation is to hear the calling of God and live accordingly. According to Paul and the entire message of the Scriptures, every single believer is called by the voice of God to do his work.

Adam and Eve were called to cultivate the garden.

Nehemiah was called by God to manage the rebuilding of Jerusalem.

The disciples were common men called to follow Jesus and later build his church.

You are the work of God's hands, called to be like him in bringing life about in our world and bringing order to chaos. Whether you are a teacher, missionary, nurse, pastor, writer, laborer or manager: You have a calling from God to do his work in the world.

CREATED FOR GOOD WORKS

Not only are you the work of God, you have been created for good work. Even before he saved you, God had your good work in mind. Your good works did not save you, but make no mistake, good works will be the result.

As the ESV Study Bible summarizes: "Salvation is not based on works, but the good works Christians do are the result and consequence of God's new creation work in them."

How should you think about your works? Is there a contradiction here? Not one bit!

You exist entirely by grace, yet you also exist to do great things for God's kingdom! This doesn't mean you now can boast of your work, but in your weakness, as the work of God, your work demonstrates the grace of God.

GOD'S POWER IS
ATTRACTED TO WEAKNESS.
HIS GRACE COMES RUNNING
TO THOSE IN NEED...
THE EMPTIER WE ARE,
THE MORE OF HIS GRACE
WE CAN RECEIVE.
THE WEAKER WE ARE,
THE MORE OF HIS STRENGTH
WE CAN DISCOVER.

- KYLE IDLEMAN -

A VOCATION OF GRACE

So what is your vocation? What is your calling in life? How will your life demonstrate the eternal grace of God?

Your nine-to-five job is certainly part of your vocation, but there's more to it than that — your good works have been "prepared in advance" for you to walk in. From before the beginning of time, God planned you to demonstrate his grace (Ephesians 1:11-12).

So how does God's grace relate to the following areas of your life? How do you hear grace "calling" in:

YOUR WORK   YOUR FAMILY

YOUR FREE
TIME

YOUR CHURCH

YOUR FRIENDS

YOUR FINANCES

YOUR FUTURE

Remember, you don't have to do all these things perfectly. There is grace — the pressure is off!

But in his grace, God equips you to let his power be seen in every aspect of your life. Even in your weakness his grace is on full display!

This is incredible to all who hear it: You have been made alive; you belong to God; you have received the gift of his grace; you were created to do the kind of good that brings God glory in the world! ■

PRAISE BE TO GOD!

HIS GRACE IS GREATER.

QUESTIONS FOR REFLECTION

CONTENT AND MEANING

HOW CAN IT BE THAT YOU HAVE BEEN SAVED "NOT BY WORKS" (VERSE 9) BUT ALSO CREATED "TO DO GOOD WORKS" (VERSE 10)?

WHAT DOES IT MEAN THAT EACH BELIEVER HAS A HOLY VOCATION? WHAT ARE THE ELEMENTS OF THIS CALLING?

QUESTIONS FOR REFLECTION

MEDITATION AND APPLICATION

Read Ephesians 2:8-10 again, but this time read it more slowly, and reflect deeply on the verses' meaning for you today.

WHAT STANDS OUT TO YOU FROM THE LIST ABOVE — YOUR CALLING IN LIFE?

HOW DO YOU STRUGGLE TO BELIEVE THAT GOD CAN EQUIP YOU BY HIS GRACE TO HAVE A PROFOUND IMPACT ON THOSE AROUND YOU?

REMEMBERING YOUR OWN WEAKNESS, WHAT DOES IT LOOK LIKE TO RECEIVE GOD'S GRACE FOR YOUR GOOD WORK IN THE WORLD?

WHERE IN YOUR COMMUNITY OR CITY DO YOU SEE THE NEED FOR GOD'S STRENGTH WORKING THROUGH AN ORDINARY PERSON LIKE YOU?WHAT IS YOUR NEXT STEP?

DAY 28

REVIEW & REFLECTION

On the seventh day of each week, we're going to pause to review and reflect on the past week.

If you are behind a day or two, use this day to catch up.

If you are caught up, use this day to review the previous six days' notes — especially all the Scripture references and stories.

Based on your week's reading and reflection, answer the following questions.

WHAT WAS THE MOST SIGNIFICANT THING I LEARNED ABOUT GOD THIS WEEK?